W9-BMY-925

AnimalWays

Eagles

AnimalWays

Eagles

TOM WARHOL AND CHRIS REITER

BENCHMARK BOOKS

MARSHALL CAVENDISH
NEW YORK

With thanks to Dr. Dan Wharton, director of the Central Park Wildlife Center, for his expert reading of this manuscript.

Benchmark Books
Marshall Cavendish
99 White Plains Road
Tarrytown, NY 10591-9001
www.marshallcavendish.com

All Internet sites were available and accurate when sent to press.

Library of Congress Cataloging-in-Publication Data
Warhol, Tom.
Eagles / by Tom Warhol and Chris Reiter.
p. cm. — (Animalways)
Includes bibliographical references (p.) and index.
Contents: Eagles, honored and feared — Eagle origins — The family of eagles — How eagles work — Flight, hunting, and migration — Eagles making eagles — The fate of eagles.
ISBN 0-7614-1578-5
1. Eagles—Juvenile literature. [1. Eagles.] I. Reiter, Chris. II. Title. III. Series.
QL696.F32W35   2003   598.9′42—dc21   2002155814

Photo Research by Candlepants Incorporated

Cover Photo: Corbis/Martin Harvey; Gallo Images

The photographs in this book are used by permission and through the courtesy of: *Corbis*: Terry W. Eggers, 2; Pete Saloutos, 9; Adam Woolfitt, 11; Historical Picture Archives, 13; Digital Image, original image NASA, 15; Bettmann, 17, 75; Bill Ross, 19; Jim Zuckerman, 21; David A. Northcott, 22; James L. Amos, 23; Robert and Lorri Franz, 31; William Manning, 35; Jeff Vanuga, 36; Tony Wilson, 39; Naturfoto, 41; Reuters NewMedia, Inc., 43; Joe McDonald, 47; Eric and David Hosking, 48, 51; Joseph Sohm; Visions of America, 53; W. Perry Conway, 55, 69, 96; Staffan Widstrand, 59; Philip Richardson, Gallo Images, 61; Ron Sanford, 62; Wolfgang Kaehler, 65; Kennan Ward, 68, 71, 82; Stuart Westmorland, 72; Eric and David Hosking, 77; Wally McNamee, 80, 94; Galen Rowell, 83; Ron Sanford, 85; Layne Kennedy, 87; Lynda Richardson, 90; Robert Patrick/Sygma, 92; Christopher Loviny, 99; AFP, back cover; *Art Resource, NY*: Reunion des Museo Nationaux, 12; Werner Forman, 88; *Photo Researcher*: Chris Butler/Science Photo Library, 24, 25; Science Photo Library, 27; Tom McHugh, 28. *Wendy Shattil/Bob Rozinski*: 54.

Printed in China

1 3 5 6 4 2

Contents

1 Eagles Honored and Feared   8
Messengers of the Gods • Bald Eagle: Symbol of the U.S.A.
• Eagles in Native American Culture

2 Eagle Origins   20
How Old Are They? • Close Relatives: Lizards?
• *Archaeopteryx*: The First Bird?

3 The Family of Eagles   30
Classification • Eagle Groups

4 How Eagles Work   50
Eagle Anatomy • Metabolism • Plumage, Size, and Sex

5 Flight, Hunting, and Migration   64
Masters of Flight • What Do Eagles Eat? • Two Homes

6 The Life Cycle   74
Courtship • Nest Building • Mating • Raising Young
• On Their Own

7 The Fate of Eagles   84
Threats to Eagles • Protection of Endangered Eagles
• Endangered Eagles

GLOSSARY 101 · SPECIES CHECKLIST 104 · FURTHER RESEARCH 107
· BIBLIOGRAPHY 108 · INDEX 110

HERE ARE SOME OF THE MAIN PHYLA, CLASSES, AND ORDERS, WITH PHOTOGRAPHS OF
A TYPICAL ANIMAL FROM EACH GROUP.

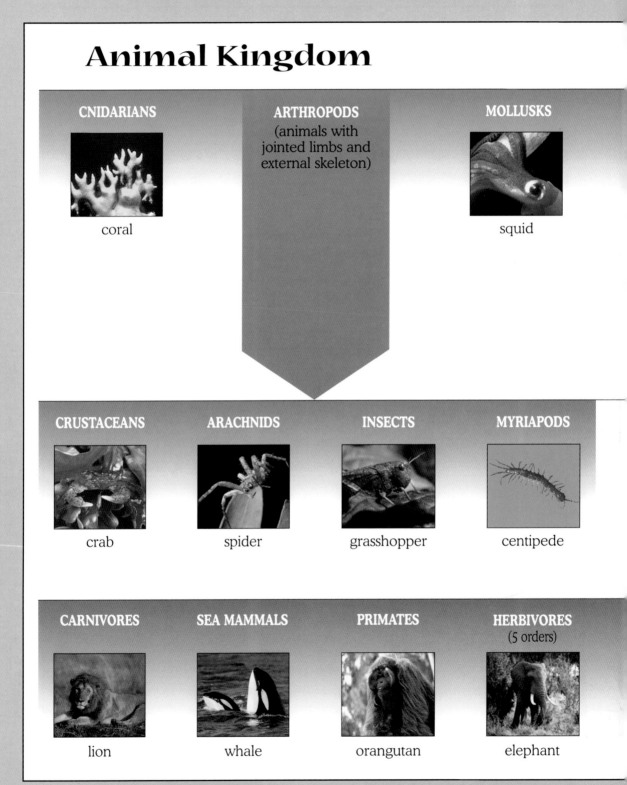

Animal Kingdom

CNIDARIANS

coral

ARTHROPODS
(animals with
jointed limbs and
external skeleton)

MOLLUSKS

squid

CRUSTACEANS

crab

ARACHNIDS

spider

INSECTS

grasshopper

MYRIAPODS

centipede

CARNIVORES

lion

SEA MAMMALS

whale

PRIMATES

orangutan

HERBIVORES
(5 orders)

elephant

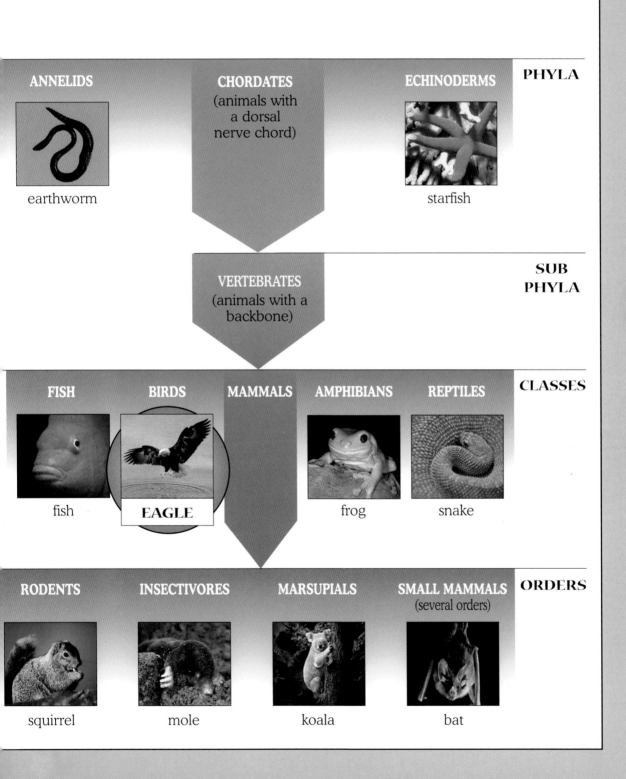

PHYLA

ANNELIDS

earthworm

CHORDATES
(animals with
a dorsal
nerve chord)

ECHINODERMS

starfish

SUB PHYLA

VERTEBRATES
(animals with a
backbone)

CLASSES

FISH

fish

BIRDS

EAGLE

MAMMALS

AMPHIBIANS

frog

REPTILES

snake

ORDERS

RODENTS

squirrel

INSECTIVORES

mole

MARSUPIALS

koala

SMALL MAMMALS
(several orders)

bat

1

Eagles Honored and Feared

Perched atop a dead tree along the shore of a slow-moving river, the massive, white-headed bird scans the water with its keen yellow eyes. Behind it, in a nest large enough for a young adult person to lie down comfortably, two small, downy, three-week-old chicks call out for food. Suddenly the mother eagle spots a large trout swimming in a shallow, shady pool. In one quick, smooth movement it pushes off with its strong feet and spreads its broad wings. Gliding just above the surface of the river, the eagle plunges its strong, sharp talons into the water, snatches the fish, and banks up and away toward its hungry chicks.

Back at the nest the eagle strips the muscular flesh from the trout and gives it to its brood. The chicks devour the meat, pulling it apart with their sharply curved beaks and swallowing large chunks. The meal satisfies the chicks for only a short while. They are soon hungry again; these young bald eagles have lots

BALD EAGLES SOAR HIGH ABOVE THE SURFACE OF THE WATER BEFORE DIVING DOWN TO GRAB A FISH.

of growing to do. Their mother weighs 14 pounds (6.35 kg) and has a wingspan of almost 6 feet (1.82 m). She can carry her own weight in her talons and see the movements of fish or other prey from a mile away. The mother eagle's powerful wings carry it thousands of feet above Earth. It will take a year or two for the chicks to match their mother's size and skill, but within eight months of their hatching they must be strong enough to fly hundreds or possibly even thousands of miles to their wintering grounds.

Many young bald eagles do not survive this trip. Life in the wild can be harsh; up to 80 percent of all eagles die within their first year. But eagles adapt well. They learn to glide on swirling currents of air and swoop down on unsuspecting prey. The daily quest for food sharpens their senses and hones their hunting skills. Over millions of years their interactions with the world's various habitats have shaped the magnificent forms of the many different eagle species. From the harpy eagle's 8-foot (2.4-m) wingspan to the golden eagle's 120-mile-per-hour (193-kph) glide to the bald eagle's bright white head and tail feathers, the eagle is the picture of boldness, tenacity, and strength—a true survivor and a wonder to behold.

Messengers of the Gods

The strength and agility of eagles has long inspired worship, study, and fear. All over the world, for thousands of years, they have been powerful cultural symbols. The oldest known image of an eagle was made in about 3000 B.C. by one of the earliest human cultures, the ancient Sumerians. Because eagles soar so high, the Sumerians and many other cultures believed that eagles carried people's souls to heaven. The Romans, for example, hid an eagle on the funeral pyre of the emperor Augustus when he died in A.D. 14, releasing it as the pyre burned. This

EAGLES WERE COMMONLY DEPICTED IN ANCIENT ART AND ARE OFTEN CONSIDERED
SYMBOLS OF GREAT POWER, AS IN THIS STONE EAGLE HEAD TOPPLED FROM A HUGE
STATUE, ONE OF MANY MADE AROUND 50 B.C. TO MARK A ROYAL BURIAL SITE ON
MOUNT NIMROD IN TURKEY.

began a tradition among Roman rulers that lasted for 250 years.
The emperors were not alone in revering eagles. When the
great Roman legions rode into battle, the standard bearer, or
aquilifer, carried a standard, or staff, topped by the image of the
imperial eagle. Romans also believed that a gifted person,
known as an auspex, could tell the future by watching eagles fly.

The eagle is prominent in classical mythology. In Roman

myth the eagle is the companion of Jupiter, and in Greek myth, it accompanies Zeus and carries thunderbolts for the gods. Although today we know that eagles do not really carry thunderbolts, in ancient times people thought living creatures had many unusual powers. The Greeks believed that eagles, because of their connection to the gods, were immune to lightning. Farmers buried eagle wings in their fields to keep storms away.

In some mythological stories, gods and humans were transformed into eagles. One myth tells how Zeus took the form of an eagle so he could carry off the beautiful young man Ganymede to be cupbearer to the gods. In another tale the goddess Hera turned King Meropes into an eagle. It was said that one of these mythic eagles may have flown into the night sky and become

THIS VESSEL DEPICTS ZEUS, THE FATHER OF ALL GREEK GODS, HOLDING THUNDERBOLTS IN ONE HAND AND AN EAGLE IN THE OTHER.

the constellation Aquila, which takes its name from the Latin word for *eagle*. Aquila is a pitchfork-shaped group of stars seen in the Northern Hemisphere. It has been recognized as an eagle shape for at least 3,500 years.

Eagles have inspired many mythical creatures, too. The griffin was a protective creature with the head and wings of an eagle and the body of a lion. It was an important figure in Greek myth, but it also appeared in other cultures from the time of ancient Mesopotamia to the Middle Ages. Ishtar, an animal in Assyrian myth associated with immortality and the sun, was the opposite of the griffin; it had the head of a lion and the body of an eagle. In the story of Sinbad, the legendary sailor meets the roc, a giant eagle from Middle Eastern mythology that could sink its talons

THE GRIFFIN, A PROTECTIVE MYTHOLOGICAL FIGURE IMPORTANT IN MANY ANCIENT CULTURES, HAD THE HEAD AND WINGS OF AN EAGLE AND THE BODY OF A LION. THIS IS A DANISH MARITIME FLAG, CA. 1819.

into the backs of elephants and carry them away. In one of the books of the Christian Bible, God is compared to an eagle and called Rock. Eagles, in fact, appear quite often in the Bible, as animals to be both feared and admired.

Eagles—especially golden eagles—were so revered by Europeans in the Middle Ages that they were brought by noblemen on military campaigns, used as gifts to seal treaties, and paid as ransom for kidnapped princes. Yet, just as in the Bible, the admiration of eagles has often been accompanied by a measure of fear. There are many legends and folktales, even today, that describe eagles carrying off children. Some people have hunted eagles because they believed that the birds destroy livestock, such as sheep and calves, and wild game, such as pheasants. While eagles may feed on sick or dead animals, they are not the sheep killers that some ranchers think. And reports of eagles carrying off babies and small children are false. Even though eagles are very strong animals, human prey is not on their menu.

Today the symbol of the eagle is still common. There is an eagle on the Mexican flag. The bald eagle graces the coat of arms of the state of Mississippi. Sports teams like the eagle's tough image, too. The National Football League has the Philadelphia Eagles; minor league hockey has Salt Lake City's Golden Eagles; and in college sports, many athletic teams use eagles as mascots. Even more obvious are the bald eagles we see every day on coins and stamps and business logos. And sometimes the great bird still stands for something larger than life. When the United States sent a mission to the moon in 1969, the lunar lander, piloted by Neil Armstrong, was named the Eagle. As the ship touched down, Armstrong radioed back to mission control. "Houston, Tranquility Base here," he said. "The Eagle has landed."

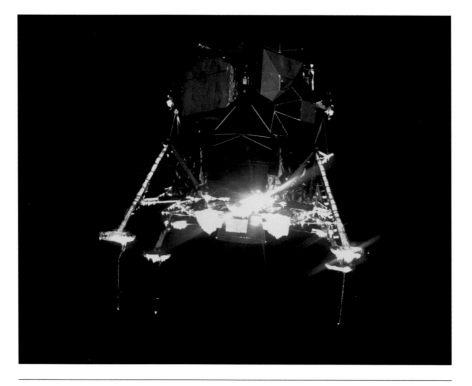

THE LUNAR MODULE PILOTED BY NEAL ARMSTRONG AND BUZZ ALDRIN FROM THE *APOLLO 11* SPACECRAFT IN 1969 WAS NAMED THE *EAGLE*.

Bald Eagle: Symbol of the U.S.A.

An eagle, of course, is also the symbol of the United States. The bald eagle is the national bird and appears on the Presidential Seal as well as the official seals of the vice pesident, the Speaker of the House of Representatives, the Senate, and the Supreme Court. It is found on U.S. quarters, half-dollars, and dollar bills. It is also a symbol for many organizations and companies: the American and National Baseball Leagues, the National Rifle Association, Anheuser-Busch brewery, Harley-Davidson motorcycles, and many more. It is hard to go a day without seeing the bald eagle used as a symbol for something.

How did this all come about? After the American colonies declared independence from Great Britain in 1776, the founders of the United States decided that they needed a symbol of the new nation to stamp on official paperwork. So the Continental Congress asked Thomas Jefferson, Benjamin Franklin, and John Adams to come up with one. After six years of debating and appointing different committees, the great leaders gave their ideas to Charles Thompson, the secretary of the Congress. One of the suggested symbols was a white eagle, which Thompson used to create the basis of the American bald eagle design we know today.

On June 20, 1782, the Continental Congress adopted a slightly altered version of Thompson's design as the Great Seal of the United States. The bald eagle sits in the center of the seal with a red- and white-striped shield on its chest, holding the olive branch of peace in one talon and the arrows of war in the other. Its head is surrounded by a cluster of thirteen stars (for the thirteen original colonies) and its beak holds a banner that reads *E Pluribus Unum*, which is Latin for "Out of Many, One."

Eagles in Native American Culture

Native American cultures have also long honored and worshipped eagles, which were believed to carry prayers to the Creator. The golden eagle was the eagle most often used as a symbol of spiritual power by Native Americans. It has also been used as a symbol of peace and of war and as the inspiration for the eagle dances of many North American tribes.

Eagle feathers were used to make headdresses, shield decorations, dance costumes, and many other items. They were also worn in the hair as marks of identity; the placement of the feather on the head and the markings on the feather let others

THE GREAT SEAL WAS ADOPTED AS THE SYMBOL OF THE UNITED STATES IN 1782. THE BALD EAGLE HOLDS THE ARROWS OF WAR AND THE OLIVE BRANCH OF PEACE IN ITS TALONS, AND THE BANNER READING *E PLURIBUS UNUM* ("OUT OF MANY, ONE") FLIES FROM ITS BEAK.

know who the wearer was and what he had done in his life. Other parts of the eagle were used by medicine men for a variety of purposes. Eagle wing bones, for example, were used to suck disease out of sick people's bodies. Plains Indians made whistles out of the wing bones.

Many Native American myths involve giant eagles that were brought down to size. In a Jicarilla Apache legend, the hero Jonaya'iyan hides in an elk skin and is carried to the dangerous eagles' nest. He kills the two adults and hits their chicks

FALCONRY

Falconry is the practice of keeping and training raptors to hunt and kill game, like birds, rabbits, and squirrels. People have been using birds to hunt for 4,000 years. In Europe in the Middle Ages, falconry was a sport of the nobility. It was the best way to catch birds, but not the easiest way to get food, since housing and training birds was very time-consuming and expensive.

The kinds of raptors a falconer flew showed his social rank. The king, princes, and noblemen flew expert fliers and killers such as the gyrfalcon and the peregrine falcon. But the only person who could fly the golden eagle was the emperor. Golden eagles were considered the best bird for falconry, but because of their huge size and strength they were very difficult and even dangerous to work with.

Falconry was more important in Asia, where teams of golden eagles were flown together to capture deer, antelope, and wolves. Marco Polo, the famous explorer of the East, told in 1276 how the Mongol emperor Kublai Khan went hunting with 500 raptors, which were cared for by 10,000 falconers.

Today most people working with raptors for falconry use smaller, more easily trained birds like kestrels, merlins, or Harris's hawks.

on the heads, stunting their growth so they won't be a danger to people anymore. This explained to the Jicarilla Apache why eagles are the size they are today.

There are also legends that show the eagle as a benevolent creature. In the Southwest the golden eagle inspired the Thunderbird, who was believed to be the Great Spirit. It lived in the heavens and caused thunder by flying. Eagles can also be

Native Americans revere the eagle and consider it to be a powerful figure. They often use it in their art. An example is the bald eagle head on this totem pole, made by the Tlingit tribe of the Pacific Northwest.

found in Native American art, especially that of tribes of the Pacific Northwest, who use eagle imagery on their totem poles and other artwork.

2

Eagle Origins

How Old Are They?

The ancestors of eagles have been around a long time. Toothed birds and water birds, the first birds to evolve, appear in the fossil record during the Mesozoic era in the Cretaceous period, which began about 144 million years ago and lasted until about 66 million years ago. During the Tertiary period in the next era, the Cenozoic, our current geologic time, the number of birds really began to increase. Eagles began to develop around 36 million years ago in the Oligocene epoch. The first were booted eagles like the golden eagle, which had a "boot" of feathers below the knee, and fish eagles like the bald eagle, which caught and ate fish.

Close Relatives: Lizards?

Scientists who study the origins of life can trace all of Earth's creatures back to tiny single-celled organisms that lived in the

MODERN BIRDS AND REPTILES, LIKE THIS CHAMELEON FROM MADAGASCAR, ARE REPRESENTATIVES OF DIVERGENT EVOLUTIONARY PATHS THAT BRANCHED OFF FROM DINOSAURS.

THE SCALES OF THIS GREEN SPINY LIZARD FROM SOUTH AMERICA ARE MADE OF THE SAME MATERIAL AS FEATHERS. SCIENTISTS SAY FEATHERS EVOLVED FROM SCALES AS REPTILES TOOK TO THE AIR.

ancient seas. From those simple creatures, thousands of diverse forms emerged over millions of years, branching out into many different classes of animals, from spiders to frogs to mammal species as varied as the whale and the bat. We could say that each class of animals has a family tree—including birds. How did they evolve?

There are two main theories of bird evolution, but they both agree on one thing: birds evolved from reptiles (like our modern lizards and snakes). It may sound strange, but there are very similar features shared by both groups of animals, from their skeletons to the eggs they lay to their blood cells. And the scales on the legs of birds are also very much like the scales on the bodies of reptiles. In fact, evolutionary biologists believe that feathers are simply modified reptilian scales.

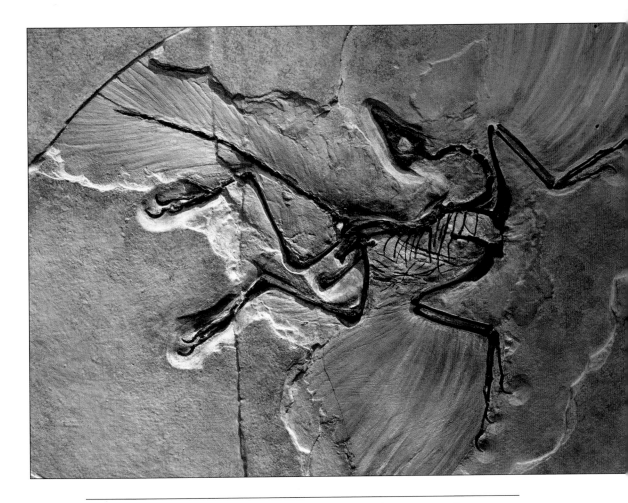

THIS FOSSIL SPECIMEN OF *ARCHAEOPTERYX*, FOUND NEAR BLUMENBERG, GERMANY, IN 1877, IS THOUGHT TO BE ONE OF THE EARLIEST ANCESTORS OF BIRDS AND WAS ALIVE AROUND 150 MILLION YEARS AGO.

Tyrannosaurus Rex was a theropod, one of the groups of dinosaurs from which birds may have descended.

The two theories suggest that birds evolved either from a group of reptiles called thecodonts or, millions of years later, from a group of dinosaurs called theropods. Both of these groups lived during the Mesozoic era, between about 245 million and 65 million years ago. Theropods included dinosaurs as large as *Tyrannosaurus rex* and as small as modern iguanas.

COMPSOGNATHUS, A THEROPOD DINOSAUR, HAD SIMILAR, BIRDLIKE SKELETAL FEATURES TO ARCHAEOPTERYX AND MAY HAVE BEEN AN EVEN EARLIER ANCESTOR OF BIRDS.

Thecodonts are the ancestors of crocodiles, although many of them were very different from our modern crocodiles. Some even lived in trees. If birds evolved from thecodonts, they were around much earlier than if they evolved from theropods. The theropod theory has one important thing going for it, though. The fossil of a small theropod called *Compsognathus* was found in a limestone quarry in Germany. This creature seems to have skeletal features very similar to those of another important fossil found preserved there: *Archaeopteryx*.

Archaeopteryx: The First Bird?

The scientists who looked at the first few fossilized specimens of *Archaeopteryx*, which were found in the Bavarian quarry in 1861, were not sure what they were looking at. There was clearly the impression of reptilian skin, but there was also something that did not make sense on a reptile—feathers! The creature was named *Archaeopteryx lithographica*. *Archios* means "ancient," and *pteryx* means "wing." *Lithos* means "stone," and *graphikos* means "to write"; the quarry where the specimens were found supplied stones for making lithographic prints. Scientists eventually discovered that these fossils of *Archaeopteryx* were formed during the Jurassic period, about 150 million years ago.

This creature seemed to be the link between birds and reptiles that scientists had been looking for. It had a blunt nose, a skull, teeth, a skeleton, claws, and a long tail similar to that of a reptile. The most obvious birdlike characteristics were the feathers covering the body, tail, and wings. *Archaeopteryx* also had a wishbone, or furcula, the bone that anchors the flight muscles of birds. It could run on the ground, leap, and glide between large branches of trees, but it could also probably fly by flapping its wings.

Archaeopteryx, about the size of a crow, is considered to be the earliest known ancestor of modern birds and the link between birds and reptiles. Note the feathers and birdlike legs.

Archaeopteryx became extinct with the dinosaurs at the end of the Cretaceous period around 65 million years ago. While this was a tragedy for the animals that died, many others survived. With less competition for food and habitat, these lucky survivors were able to expand their range and continue to evolve over millions of years. By the time of the Pleistocene epoch, about 2 million years ago, huge creatures like the mammoth and herds of horses and bison were roaming the land, and

HAAST'S EAGLE

An eagle that became extinct much more recently was Haast's eagle. At the time of its extinction, during the 1700s, it was the world's largest eagle, weighing about 30 pounds (13.6 kg). Haast's eagle lived on the New Zealand islands and fed on the large eggs and young of a flightless bird called the moa, which was about 8 to 9 feet (2.4 to 2.7 m) tall. When the Maori people arrived to colonize the island about 1,000 years ago, they hunted the moas, too. Within 600 years, the moas and the eagles were extinct.

UP UNTIL THE 1700S, THE EGGS AND YOUNG OF GIANT MOAS, A GROUP OF LARGE FLIGHTLESS BIRDS FROM NEW ZEALAND, WERE A FAVORITE PREY OF THE 30-POUND (13.6-KG) HAAST'S EAGLE.

Era	Period	Epoch	Years Ago	Event
Cenozoic	Quatenary	Holocene	10,000	Two North American eagles left alive Mass extinction, including teratorns, mammoths, bison, and five eagle species
		Pleistocene		
			2 million	All modern bird genera established
	Tertiary	Pliocene	5 million	Beginning of Ice Ages
		Miocene	24 million	
		Oligocene	37 million	Booted and fish eagles evolve
		Eocene	58 million	First appearance of raptorlike birds
		Paleocene	65 million	Bird diversity expands Mass extinction killing dinosaurs and leaving many birds
Mesozoic	Cretaceous		144 million	Waterbirds and toothed birds evolve
	Jurassic		150 million	*Archaeopteryx* and *Compsognathus* alive
			208 million	
	Triassic		225 million 245 million	Theropods evolve Thecodonts evolve
Paleozoic			570 million	
Precambrian Time			4.6 billion	

large birds like teratorns were soaring through the skies. These were like today's condors, but they were as tall as a man and had wingspans of up to twenty-five feet (7.6 m)! There were also seven species of eagles living in North America during this time. The next mass extinction, at the end of the Pleistocene epoch, about 10,000 years ago, killed off many of these animals and all but two of the eagle species living in North America.

3

The Family of Eagles

There are many different species of birds in the world—more than nine thousand. The family of eagles is part of a smaller group of birds called raptors, or birds of prey. What makes a raptor a raptor? Ornithologists, scientists who study birds, are still trying to answer that question, but the main characteristics of raptors are: they are carnivorous, meaning they catch and eat live animals, called their prey; they are very large (actually, they are some of the largest flying birds in the world); they have strong, sharp talons, or claws, and beaks for catching and tearing apart prey; and they have keen eyesight for spotting it. Hawks, falcons, vultures, kites, owls, and eagles are all part of the raptor group.

Classification

It is hard to keep all these birds straight; harder still to grasp the names of the thousands of other species of animals, plants,

WHILE EAGLES ARE USUALLY NOT SOCIAL ANIMALS, EXCEPT WHEN BREEDING, BALD EAGLES DO CONGREGATE IN LARGE NUMBERS IN AREAS WHERE FOOD IS PLENTIFUL.

mushrooms, bacteria, and microorganisms that inhabit Earth, especially when people in different parts of the world call the same animal by different names. To help classify and understand living things, scientists use a system developed by Carolus Linnaeus in the eighteenth century. Linnaeus used Latin for the names of every plant and animal so his fellow scientists in different European countries could all use the same names and understand one another.

This form of classification, called a taxonomic system, puts all living things into categories, starting with the broadest one, kingdom, and ending with the most specific, species. Raptors are in the kingdom Animalia (distinguishing them from plants, bacteria, and fungi), the phylum Chordata (meaning they have spinal cords), and the class Aves (identifying them as birds). They are then divided into two orders, Strigiformes (which includes the nocturnal, or nighttime-hunting raptors—owls) and Falconiformes (which includes the diurnal, or daytime-hunting raptors—hawks, eagles, kites, falcons, and Old World vultures). The Falconiformes order contains three families, the Cathartidae (New World, or American, vultures), the Falconidae (falcons) and Accipitridae (all other diurnal raptors, including eagles). After this, eagles are separated into different genera (for example, the genus Aquila), which are groups of closely related species, and then they are each given their own species names. A species is a group of organisms with common characteristics that separate them from all other organisms. This is considered to be the finest level of classification, although some specialists break things down further into subspecies.

The genus name is always capitalized, and the species always begins with a lowercase letter. Both names are italicized. For example, the golden eagle's scientific name is *Aquila chrysaetos*.

There are sixty-four different species of eagles in the world in twenty-two different genera. They vary in size from falcon-sized birds, like the Ayres' hawk-eagle, which weighs only 1.5 to 2 pounds (0.7 to 0.9 kg), to the largest raptor in the world, the harpy eagle. Females of this species can reach a weight of 20 pounds (9 kg) and have a wingspan of nearly 8 feet (2.4 m).

Eagles live on every continent except Antarctica, in diverse habitats such as forests, mountains, arctic barrens, deserts, grasslands, and coastal and lake areas. Two species of eagle live in North America: the bald eagle resides only on the North American continent; the golden eagle's territory is the whole Northern Hemisphere. Bald and golden eagles occupy different habitats and prefer different prey, so they do not compete with each other for food and homes. The bald eagle is a fish eagle, so it prefers to live and hunt near large bodies of water. The golden eagle is a booted eagle that prefers mountainous habitat and feeds on mammals and carrion, or dead animals. Some eagles migrate, or move from a winter home to a summer home where they breed, or raise young.

To make it easier to study eagles, they have been divided into four different groups based on their morphology—their shape—and their habits.

Booted Eagles. Booted eagles get their name from their feathered tarsi, which are their legs below the ankle. No other eagle group has these. Booted eagles can be as large as 36 inches (91 cm) from head to tip of tail and can weigh up to 14 pounds (6.4 kg). Many booted eagles look similar to the golden eagle, being mostly brown or black with some white streaking or striping. This is the largest group of eagles, with thirty-three species in

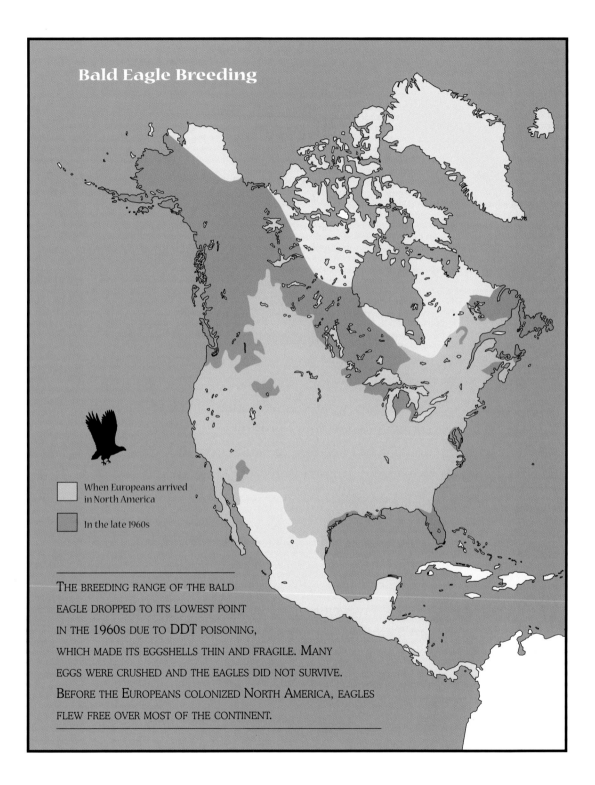

Bald Eagle Breeding

When Europeans arrived
in North America

In the late 1960s

THE BREEDING RANGE OF THE BALD
EAGLE DROPPED TO ITS LOWEST POINT
IN THE 1960S DUE TO DDT POISONING,
WHICH MADE ITS EGGSHELLS THIN AND FRAGILE. MANY
EGGS WERE CRUSHED AND THE EAGLES DID NOT SURVIVE.
BEFORE THE EUROPEANS COLONIZED NORTH AMERICA, EAGLES
FLEW FREE OVER MOST OF THE CONTINENT.

THE DIET OF EAGLES INCLUDES MOST LIVING CREATURES THAT THEY CAN CATCH, EVEN DANGEROUS PREY LIKE THIS SPITTING COBRA. SNAKES ARE THE MAIN PREY OF SNAKE EAGLES, BUT OTHERS, LIKE THIS TAWNY EAGLE (A BOOTED EAGLE) WILL ALSO CONSUME THEM.

nine genera. Most booted eagles live in Europe, Asia, and Africa. They live inland and eat birds, carrion, and small mammals like mice, rabbits, and skunks. They build large nests, up to ten feet (3 m) across and twelve feet (3.6 m) deep, in trees or sometimes on cliffs. They lay from one to three eggs per breeding season.

The golden eagle is one of the most numerous eagles in the world and, as a species, has one of the biggest ranges. Golden eagles live in mountainous territory all over the Northern Hemisphere—in North America, Greenland, Europe, Asia, and as far south as Mexico, northern Africa, and the

Himalayan mountains of India and Tibet. The golden eagles that live in the far northern and southern parts of their range migrate. The home range for an individual or pair of eagles can be between 35 and 200 square miles (91 and 518 km^2), depending on the habitat.

Golden eagles are mostly dark brown, but the feathers on the crown, or top of their heads, and nape, or back of their necks, are a brownish orange color. The belly and legs are a paler brown than the back. Their eyes are hazel, their feet and cere, or unfeathered skin around their face, are yellow, and their bill and talons are black. They range in size from 30 to 36 inches

GOLDEN EAGLES SOAR GRACEFULLY OVER THE OPEN AND MOUNTAINOUS COUNTRY OF THE AMERICAN WEST, BUT THEY ARE ALSO FOUND IN SIMILAR HABITATS ALL OVER THE NORTHERN HEMISPHERE.

(76 to 91cm) from head to tail and in weight from 7 to 13 pounds (3 to 6 kg). Their wingspan is between 6 and 7 feet (about 2 m).

In the western United States, a golden eagle soaring high over the mountains, looking for food, is not an unusual sight. Golden Eagles are very strong, graceful fliers, barely wavering, even in 100-mile-per-hour (161-kph) winds, and they have been estimated to glide as fast as 120 mph (193 kph). They hunt from the air, sometimes stooping down onto prey even faster, perhaps 150 to 200 mph (241 to 322 kph)! Though golden eagles can kill a 15-pound (6.8-kg) deer fawn, they sometimes eat carrion, even when the hunting is good; in the winter, it is the staple of their diet.

The range of the beautiful ornate hawk-eagle extends from the humid tropics of central Mexico down to northern Argentina and Paraguay in South America. Not much is known about this bird since it is fairly secretive, spending most of its time in the forest. It used to be a fairly common bird, but with the massive cutting of South America's forests for farming, ranching, and lumber, it is threatened.

Above its bright orange eyes, the ornate hawk-eagle has a very striking black crest on the crown of its head. Some people think the position of the crest may suggest the bird's mood. Around its neck and in patches on its breast are bright chestnut-colored feathers, which frame a pure white throat edged in black stripes and spots. Below, its chest is white with black bars. It measures 21 to 25 inches (53 to 64 cm) from head to tail. Males weigh about 2 pounds (0.9 kg); females weigh from 3 to 3.5 pounds (1.4 to 1.6 kg).

Ornate hawk-eagles feed on large ground birds like chacha-lacas, guans, and quails, as well as little blue herons. Their calls include a high-pitched scream, and one researcher says that while perched and hunting, these birds cry like a snarling 100-pound (45-kg) cat. They seem to prefer to nest in the dry season, which probably keeps the chicks safe from bugs and diseases.

Fish eagles. These large birds, up to 20 pounds (9 kg) and 40 inches (about 1 m) long, are found throughout the world except in South America. They live near large bodies of water and feed mainly on fish and water birds. Their feet are very powerful and have special tools for catching slippery fish: toes with long, sharp talons, which have grooves underneath, and spicules on the bottoms of their feet. They also have larger bills than any other eagle group. This may be because they often feed in groups. A larger, stronger bill helps them grab and tear apart food more quickly than the eagle next to them. Fish eagles do not always catch their own food; they are well known for pirating, or stealing, it from other raptors. They are usually brown or brown and white and their hatchlings are gray, brown, or white, depending on the species. There are eleven species in three genera.

The bald eagle lives along lakes, rivers, and seacoasts of the North American continent from northern Canada to Florida in the east and Alaska to Baja California in the west. The birds are migratory in the northern and southern parts of their range; some bald eagles spend the summer in Alaska and winter in Baja California, while others stay year-round in the South.

The adult bald eagle's bright white head, its yellow eyes and bill atop an evenly brown body, white tail, and yellow legs are unmistakable. First-year bald eagles are mostly all brown and may easily be mistaken for golden eagles. Female bald eagles are bigger than males, as in all raptor species. But there are also

The African fish eagle, known as "the voice of Africa" for its habit of calling for long periods, looks somewhat similar to the bald eagle, but it is much smaller.

Bald Eagle

size differences between birds depending on where they live on the continent. The bald eagles that spend the summer breeding season in the north are about 10 percent to 15 percent larger than the southern ones. The females weigh between 10 and 14 pounds (4.5 and 6.4 kg) and the males between 8 and 10 pounds

(3.6 and 4.5 kg). This larger size probably helps the birds to retain heat better. The smallest bald eagles can be found in Florida during the breeding season.

While fish is a staple of their diet, bald eagles also catch and eat waterfowl, such as ducks and herons, and mammals, such as rabbits and rats. Adults will sometimes scavenge and eat carrion—sea lions, seals, and even whales along the seacoast—but immature eagles eat it more frequently. Often they will take advantage of tides, waiting for dead and dying fish to drift to them.

The Steller's sea-eagle is one of the largest eagles in the world and by far the largest fish eagle. This handsome and powerful bird spends its time along the rocky coastline and inland forested river corridors of northeast Siberia; some birds winter in Japan and Korea. While you may see the Steller's sea-eagle

THE BEAK OF THE STELLER'S SEA-EAGLE IS LARGER AND MORE COMPRESSED THAN MANY OTHER EAGLES. ALSO, NOTE THE WHITE FEATHERS JUST ABOVE THE CERE: THESE HELP TO IDENTIFY THIS BIRD.

regularly in its home range, the population is not very large. Like the bald eagle, in the northern part of its range, the eagles gather in large numbers to feed on salmon. The southern birds are mostly solitary.

One of the most noticeable things about this impressive bird is its large but compressed beak with its sharply curved tip. With this powerful tool, the Steller's sea-eagle is able to tear into whatever prey it wishes to eat. The plumage of the adult also makes this bird unmistakable: dark brown with a white spot on the forehead; pure white shoulders, thighs, and tail; and yellow legs. The Steller's sea-eagle is also noticeable because of its noisy calling, even at night.

The largest part of the Steller's sea-eagle's diet consists of fish, but it also preys on waterbirds, seals, hares, and other mammals, even predators such as foxes. These eagles also take advantage of stranded sea life, such as crabs, fish, and mollusks. They, too, feed on carrion; immature birds can often be found in winter at slaughterhouses, feeding on offal, or waste parts, of animals.

Harpy eagles. Harpy eagles live in the dense forests of the tropics. There are six species in five genera. Four of these live in Central and South America, one on the Philippine Islands, and one in New Guinea in the South Pacific, north of Australia. Two harpy eagles, the harpy eagle (which lives in the Americas and gives its name to the group) and the Philippine eagle, are big enough and strong enough to catch and eat large animals like monkeys and sloths. The smaller solitary eagles hunt snakes and slower-moving prey like skunks. There is not much known about harpy eagles because they live in such deep forests, areas difficult to get to and travel in. Their nests are hard to watch as well because they are usually high up in very tall trees.

The harpy eagle is the largest and one of the most powerful

The impressive crest of the harpy eagle, from Central and South America, can be raised when the bird is alert or feels threatened.

eagles in the world. Its wings are shorter and rounder than those of other eagles of its size. That's because the harpy eagle needs to maneuver through the dense trees and shrubs of virgin tropical forests in Central and South America to catch its prey—monkeys and sloths. Longer wings would make it more difficult to get through tight spaces in and around trees.

Males generally weigh 9 to 10 pounds (4.1 to 4.5 kg), while females range from 15 to 20 pounds (6.8 to 9.1 kg). The harpy eagle's name refers to a monstrous creature in Greek mythology with the head and trunk of a woman and the wings, tail, and talons of a raptorlike bird. With its crest of black feathers and its light gray face, black wings, and white chest, the happy eagle can be a scary-looking bird. Its appearance and its wailing call could make anyone's skin crawl. The tarsi, as thick as a child's wrist, are thicker than those of any other raptor. The talons are also larger than those of other raptors.

Harpy eagles stay below the tree canopy, the top layer of trees, hunting monkeys, sloths, coatimundis, opossums, and raccoons in trees and on the ground. Since they are so secretive, not much is known about their breeding habits, but they seem to mate only once every other year. Nests have been observed as high as 155 feet (47 m) in tall trees.

Almost as large as the harpy, the Philippine eagle is an equally impressive and intimidating raptor. It lives on some of the larger Philippine Islands and, like the harpy, prefers dense forests. Formerly known as the Philippine monkey-eating eagle, its name was changed when researchers discovered that its main food was flying lemurs and other mammals. It does, however, eat monkeys and large birds. Groups of birds will mob this raptor to drive it away, and monkeys get very nervous and noisy when the Philippine eagle is around. This large eagle rarely soars, spending most of its time flying quietly from perch to perch in the forest.

Like other harpy eagles, the Philippine eagle has a crest, though it is much larger, and the feathers stand up like a lion's mane. The plumes are white with dark brown streaks. Its underside is white and its thighs are streaked brown, while the back is all brown. The bill is very large and compressed like the Steller's sea-eagle, and the tarsi and talons are almost as large as those of the harpy eagle.

Snake eagles. Snake eagles are small- to medium-sized eagles, measuring from 17 to 27 inches (43 to 69 cm) long and weighing from 1.5 to 6.5 pounds (0.7 to 3 kg). Like the harpy eagles, snake eagles also have crests on their heads. You can find them in savannas and open forests of tropical Asia, Australia, Europe, and Africa. They prefer the open country because that's where their main prey—snakes—live. Their toes are strong and thick and their legs and toes are covered with very tough scales to help protect them from bites. Snake eagles will even eat venomous snakes. They disable the snake by breaking its back with their beaks, then they crush the head so it will not get caught when they swallow the snake whole, headfirst. There are fourteen species of snake eagles in five genera.

The relatively small, beautifully marked crested serpent eagles call loudly as they soar over their year-round homes in the tropical forests of southern Asia, Indonesia, and the Philippines. Each bird's home range is only about 2 square miles (5.2 km^2). There are many different subspecies, or closely related species, of this eagle. Most of them are similar in appearance: reddish brown breast, thighs, undertail, and underwings, spotted with small white dots ringed with black; dark brown back; and a black crest streaked with white. They feed on reptiles such as tree snakes, and they will even pick up dead snakes from the ground. Pairs of crested serpent eagles stay together all year. When sitting on a nest, the protective females do not leave or abandon the nest easily.

The bateleur is a very unusual eagle and a very unusual snake eagle as well. Its colorful and distinctive plumage makes it unmistakable as it glides over the tropical grasslands of Africa. This eagle is about 24 inches long (61 cm) and weighs 4 to 7 pounds (1.8 to 3.2 kg). It spends most of its day in flight, covering an estimated 200 air miles (322 km) every day. The word *bateleur* is French for "acrobat" or "balancer," which is a good description of this eagle. It flaps its long wings quickly to get off the ground, but when it is airborne, it cruises without much effort. It is also very acrobatic in the air, weaving side to side and doing 360-degree sideways rolls.

The bateleur's plumage is mostly black and chestnut. The chestnut color covers its back in a long broad line down to the tail. The tail is very short compared with its unusually long wings. This combination allows the eagle to soar quickly. The feathers on the wings are brownish with white tips. The cere and legs are a bright red.

The bateleur is the only snake eagle known to eat carrion regularly. It even pirates food from other birds, such as vultures, diving down onto them and striking them to scare them away from a carcass. It scavenges, picking up small, dead animals, but it also feeds on live reptiles such as tortoises and snakes and small mammals such as rats, squirrels, and hedgehogs.

Bateleur mating pairs like to build their nests in trees close to roads or over rivers. If any other creature comes too close, they get very excited and defend the nest. During nesting, however, a third bird will hang around the nest, perhaps a juvenile

Although among the smallest of eagles, snake eagles, like this black-chested snake eagle from Kenya, have very tough scales on their legs and very strong toes for catching their dangerous prey.

The beautiful plumage and distinctively colored red cere and feet of the bateleur, a snake eagle from Africa, make this eagle easy to identify in the field.

male bird from a previous nesting. This is very unusual behavior for eagles.

Unfortunately, this eagle is not as common as it once was; the bateleur occupies only 20 percent of its original habitat. The deaths of many of these birds from hunting and random killing, as well as dying from poisoned bait left for jackals, have put the bateleur in danger of extinction.

4 How Eagles Work

The qualities that make an eagle such a magnificent creature—its graceful and powerful flight, commanding presence, and hunting prowess—are largely determined by its body structure and proportions. Like all animals, the eagle's form has been shaped and honed by millions of years of evolution; as animals adapt to their surroundings, the characteristics that help them survive are passed on to their offspring. For example, the woodpeckers, bird species that eat tree-dwelling insects, developed a long, straight, sharp beak, a large and sturdy skull, and shock-absorbing muscles in the jaw. These features allow them to pound holes into trees to find their food without suffering harm from repeated impact. Eagles have found their own way to survive. They have evolved to possess the tools of an efficient flying hunter of live prey: strength, agility, piercing eyesight, and sharp tools for killing and tearing meat.

THE IMPERIAL EAGLE, *AQUILA HELIACA*, FROM ASIA AND INDIA, WAS FORMERLY CONSIDERED TO BE THE SAME SPECIES AS THE SPANISH IMPERIAL EAGLE, *AQUILA ADALBERTI*, FROM SPAIN AND NORTH AFRICA.

Eagle Anatomy

Skeleton. For such a large, active, powerful creature, an eagle's skeleton is surprisingly lightweight. A bald eagle's skeleton, for example, makes up only 7 percent of its total mass. If it were any heavier, the eagle would not be able to fly. Yet the skeleton must also be strong. The eagle's survival depends on the bird being

Eagle Skeleton

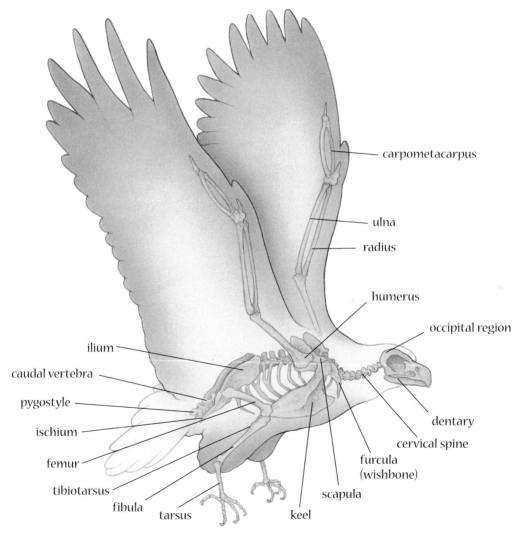

carpometacarpus

ulna

radius

humerus

occipital region

ilium

caudal vertebra

pygostyle

ischium

femur

tibiotarsus

fibula

tarsus

keel

scapula

furcula (wishbone)

cervical spine

dentary

light enough to fly and strong enough to kill its prey. Special adaptations in the eagle's bones balance these competing needs.

As in most birds, many of the bones, such as those in the wings and legs, are hollow, with criss-crossing supports that provide the stability of dense bone without its weight. The keel bone in a bird's chest needs to be big and flexible since it anchors the large, strong flight muscles. A bird's wing strokes are so powerful, in fact, that it has a special bone, the wishbone, or furcula, to keep its chest from being crushed. In addition, there are strong, elastic joints between the bones of the wing. These let a bird lock its wing in place when soaring or fold it up next to its body when perched on a tree branch.

A potentially heavy bone, the skull, is also very light. An eagle's skull is mostly made up of very large eye sockets—because eyes are very important to a hunter—and a very thin braincase.

Beak and Talons. The beak is the heaviest, densest part of an eagle's skull and is made up of bone covered by keratin, the same material that makes up their feathers. Keratin also makes up a human's fingernails, a cow's horns, and a snake's scales. Between an eagle's beak and the eyes is the cere. This bare skin

THE POWERFUL BEAK OF THE BALD EAGLE CAN EASILY TEAR INTO PREY.

helps to keep the blood and flesh of prey from sticking to the bird's face and eyes and causing infection. A brightly colored cere may also make an eagle appear more attractive to potential mates or fiercer to intruders.

An eagle's legs are covered in scales similar to those of reptiles. The lower part of the leg below the knee, the tarsometatarsus, is a long, modified foot. The foot has four toes, three facing forward and one facing back. Each toe ends in a long, curved, pointed talon, which is a claw and is an eagle's main weapon for catching and killing prey. Like the beak, the talons are made of

EAGLE TALONS ARE COMPOSED OF A TOUGH MATERIAL CALLED KERATIN AND ARE POWERFUL TOOLS FOR CRUSHING AND PIERCING THE BACK OR HEAD OF THEIR PREY.

bone covered in keratin. By using its feet instead of its beak for the kill, an eagle can avoid getting its body and face scratched, bitten, or cut. An eagle uses its beak to pluck and tear apart food once prey is dead.

BALD EAGLES USE THEIR POWERFUL TALONS FOR CATCHING AND KILLING THEIR MAIN PREY—FISH, WATERFOWL, AND SMALL MAMMALS.

The legs and feet of the various eagles have evolved differently to serve the particular needs of each species. Snake eagles have extra-thick scales on their tarsi to protect their legs from snakebites. Fish eagles have ridged scales called spicules on the bottoms of their feet to help them grab slippery fish. The tarsi of some harpy eagles are very thick and strong because these eagles catch large prey. Booted eagles have feathers that in some cases go all the way down to their toes. Scientists are not sure why this is so, but they think feathery feet may add protection or be used for display.

Eyes. The eyes of eagles are among the most highly evolved in the animal kingdom. (Hence, the term "eagle eyes.") With vision two to three times more powerful than a human's, some eagles can see their prey moving from more than a mile away.

One reason that eagles are sharp-sighted is because their

eyes are so big. In fact, their eyes are larger than those of an adult man. And they are also deep—they go way back into the eagle's head. Together, the size and depth of an eagle's eye gives it the ability to see far and focus quickly, so it can pick out prey and obstacles while hurtling through the sky or darting through deep, dense forest. And if the sun is too bright as the eagle is soaring over fields or open water looking for food, special oils in its eyes help reduce glare and increase contrast.

Each of the eagle's large eyes is encased in bone for protection, so the bird cannot actually move its eyes very much. An eagle must turn its head to look from side to side. Eagles also have a bony brow, like our own eyebrow ridge, that helps to shade and protect their eyes. When they are crashing through brush or pouncing down upon prey, a third eyelid called the nictitating membrane closes over each eye to help shield it. It is a translucent layer of skin that pulls across the eyes from front to back and also helps moisten them. All of this protection illustrates that an eagle's eyes are indeed extremely important tools.

Muscles. The eagle's flight muscles, which attach to the keel bone, are the largest muscles in an eagle's body—they equal 15 percent of the total weight of the bird. These muscles are made up of different types of muscle fibers: white fibers are used for takeoff and red fibers for flying once the bird is in the air. Different birds have different amounts of red and white fibers. Eagles and other birds that spend a lot of time in the air, either soaring or flying long distances, have more red fibers in their muscles. Ground birds like chickens, grouse, turkey, and quail have more white fibers. They use their wings for taking off suddenly and quickly and cannot usually fly very far. That's why there is mostly white meat on the breast of the chickens that people eat. If you eat duck, you will see the breast is made of dark meat; ducks use their muscles for flying long distances.

Eagle Muscles

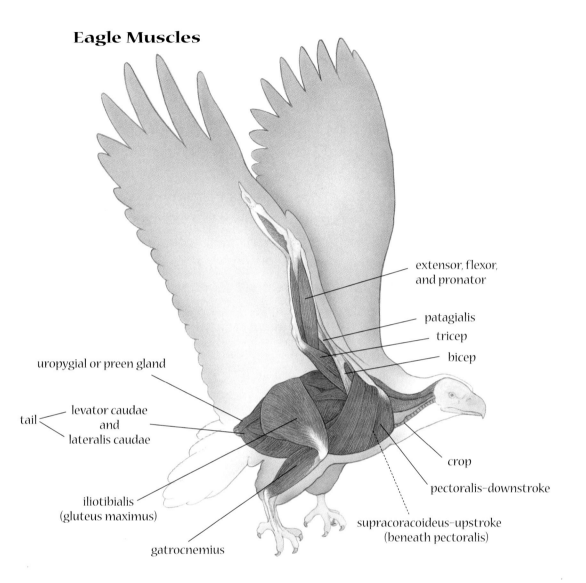

extensor, flexor, and pronator

patagialis

tricep

bicep

uropygial or preen gland

crop

levator caudae and lateralis caudae

tail

pectoralis-downstroke

iliotibialis (gluteus maximus)

supracoracoideus-upstroke (beneath pectoralis)

gatrocnemius

Metabolism

Flying uses up lots of energy. So does maintaining a body temperature of about 101 degrees Fahrenheit (38° C) and a large, fast-pumping heart. All this activity means that birds have to eat a lot to supply their bodies with enough fuel to keep working. They also digest their food quickly, so it seems that some birds are always eating, from dawn to dusk. Eagles and other large raptors tend to eat larger meals than birds that live off insects, seeds, or fruits, so they eat less often, but they eat large amounts.

Unlike most mammals, birds do not have teeth, so they cannot crush their food before swallowing. Most birds, including eagles, need to feed quickly to keep from exposing themselves to predators or competitors for long periods of time. When a bird finds food, as when an eagle makes a kill or comes upon a carcass, it may not be able to carry all it needs back to a safe place to eat. So birds "eat" quickly by storing food in their crop, a special sac in their throat. Then they fly to a safe spot such as a high branch in a tree, where the crop slowly releases food into the stomach. The crop also softens the food before it passes on to the gizzard, a hard-edged part of the stomach that does the real work of breaking down the food.

Even though birds have these special tools, not everything they swallow is digestible or nutritious. Since they eat meat but do not have a chef to prepare a nice filet, they end up swallowing bones, fur, and other bits along with the meat. While their digestive acids and their gizzards can break down food very well, they cannot dissolve everything. So most raptors regurgitate, or vomit, pellets. These are usually tight little plugs about one or two inches (2.5 or 5 cm) long—rounded, dark gray, and made up of hair and bone fragments. Sometimes you can find these on the ground. If you take them apart, you can find out what the birds have been eating.

Eagles do not drink very often; they get most of their water from their food. Also, they are able to conserve water because they do not excrete that much. Their urine is made up of uric acid, which contains less water than human urine. This is passed out of the bird's body through the cloaca, the opening also used for defecation and reproduction.

Feathers. Birds are unique animals in many ways, but what really makes a bird special is its plumage, or feather coat. Feathers have evolved to catch the air, repel water, communicate, and provide warmth and camouflage. They are made of keratin like reptile scales and arranged in overlapping layers like shingles on a roof. Although feathers are not very heavy, they weigh more than the bird's skeleton—about two-and-one-half times more.

The coat is not just a bunch of the same kinds of feathers stuck on the bird's body. There are a number of different kinds of feathers, and they have different properties and purposes. They are all made up of a stiff, hollow shaft covered by the vane. The vane consists of the softer parts of the feather that break apart when you rub them one way and smooth together when you

THESE WING FEATHERS OF A WEDGE-TAILED EAGLE SHOW THE TIPS OF THE VANE, COMPOSED OF THE DARK CENTRAL SHAFT SURROUNDED BY BARBS.

rub them the other way. The individual parts are called barbs; they have tiny little hooks called barbules that hold the barbs together and allow them to be smoothed out by the bird's beak. These feathers help deflect water and wind. At the base of the body, or contour, feathers is a layer of downy feathers that helps to keep birds warm.

Mixed in with the wing and body feathers are small feathers with long slender shafts and wispy barbs at the tip called filoplumes. These amazing feathers actually tell the other feathers what to do! In flight, for example, the bird can adjust its flight feathers based on wind conditions that are sensed by the nerves in its body through the movement of the more sensitive filoplumes.

The feathers are also connected to muscles that allow birds to move them; they can flatten their feathers to make them more aerodynamic, or less resistant to air currents, or fluff them up to keep warm. Eagles can also raise the feathers on their heads. Scientists think that eagles may raise these crests when excited or when trying to scare off intruders.

There are two kinds of wing feathers, the primaries and the secondaries. The primary feathers on the hand, or outer wing, give eagles the power to move when they stroke their wings. The secondary feathers along the arm of the wing catch the wind and keep the bird in the air.

Eagles and other birds spend a lot of time caring for their feathers, or preening, arranging them with their beaks so they are smooth, in order, and ready to fly at a moment's notice. Like human hair, feathers need to be kept moist so they do not get damaged. When birds preen, they also touch their beak to the base of their rump, getting oils from the preen glands and spreading it on their feathers to keep them strong and waterproof.

Differences Between Eagles. Many birds of the same species

To keep their feathers in good condition, birds like this tawny eagle in the
Kalahari of South Africa preen regularly, using oils from the base of
their tails.

exhibit differences in size, plumage, and shape. This difference
between the sexes is called sexual dimorphism. Females and
males of most animal species are different sizes. Usually the male
is larger than the female because he needs to defend territory
and compete for mates. Eagles and other raptors are unusual in
that the females tend to be larger than the males—this is called
reverse sexual dimorphism. Scientists argue about why this is so.
Some say that since most raptor females spend more time on

BALD EAGLE MOLTING

Bald eagles do not become mature and get their adult feathers until they are nearly five years old. They go through a series of changes from year to year.

When they are born, they are covered in a thin layer of gray, downy feathers and soon grow a fuller downy layer. During their first winter their bodies are mostly brown and their beaks are dark. In their second winter bald eagles usually have a white stomach with some dark streaks and a dark head and chest. By the third year they may have more white streaking on their undersides. Between this and the adult phase, they may have a blend of a white head with some dark feathers. Finally they look like the bald eagle we know so well—pure white head and tail, yellow beak and feet, and the rich brown body. Now they are adults and ready to mate for the first time.

IT TAKES FOUR TO FIVE YEARS FOR A BALD EAGLE TO MOLT INTO ITS ADULT PLUMAGE. THIS EAGLE IS IN ITS SECOND OR THIRD YEAR.

the eggs and around the nest, their larger size helps them protect and provide for their young. Another opinion is that the differences in size allows the mates to take advantage of different-sized food sources, reducing competition between the sexes for food and increasing the variety of prey available to the young.

When there are differences in plumage between bird sexes, the males are usually more brightly colored or have more complex plumage for courtship and display. In most species the males compete to attract the females, and the best-looking, healthiest males tend to get the mates. Raptors in general and eagles especially do not have as many differences between the sexes as many other birds.

Young eagles almost always look different from their adult parents. In many cases they go through a series of plumage changes. Immature eagles also look larger than adults. This is because their flight and tail feathers are actually longer, which may make it easier for them to learn how to fly. They will lose these longer feathers when they get their adult plumage.

But they are not finished losing feathers—even adults molt. Feathers get worn down and damaged, so they must be replaced. Eagles do this slowly, and they do not do it one at a time. If they were to replace one flight feather on the right wing, that would throw off their balance. Instead, the eagle's body knows it must replace the same feather on both wings at the same time. Many birds replace their feathers every year, but eagles may take two to three years to replace theirs.

5 Flight, Hunting, and Migration

Almost all birds fly, and many fly in characteristic ways; their body type and feathers are specially adapted for their own particular needs. Swallows are sleek and streamlined, with narrow, pointed wings that allow them to swoop and soar after insects over ponds and fields. Hummingbirds are tiny, and they move their wings rapidly in a figure-eight pattern so they can hover above a flower while they drink its nectar. Eagles, of course, are huge by comparison. Their wings are large, strong, and constructed for soaring and gliding. In spite of these differences, all birds have the same basic design.

The wings of all birds are curved downward so that, when they are flying, the air moves more quickly above the wing than below; the slower-moving air underneath helps to hold the bird aloft as it soars. Curved wings also help birds scoop the air when flapping. The tail acts as both a rudder and brake, allowing

FISH EAGLES SPEND A LOT OF TIME FLYING OR PERCHING ABOVE LAKES OR RIVERS BEFORE SWOOPING DOWN FOR THEIR PREY. THIS AFRICAN FISH EAGLE HAS CAUGHT A LARGE FISH IN THE OKAVANGO DELTA, BOTSWANA, AFRICA.

quick turns and stops. Together, these adaptations make birds supremely well suited for flight.

Masters of Flight

While most birds are gifted fliers, eagles and other raptors may be the masters of flight, able to soar and glide like no other creature on Earth.

Depending on the kind of prey they hunt, different eagle species use different kinds of flight. All birds use active flight, the hard, energy-intensive flapping that lifts them off the ground. This is hard to sustain, so eagles also rely on other kinds of flight.

The largest eagles are masters of soaring. Soaring does not involve a lot of work, and that's ideal for eagles that have a lot of ground to cover. The golden eagle and the crowned eagle spend much of their time soaring as they look for prey: the golden eagle hunts in open country with scattered vegetation, and the crowned eagle hunts over the treetops in forested Africa, looking for monkeys and other animals. They keep their wings outspread when riding thermals, the currents of warm air that rise from the ground as it is heated by the sun. Sometimes you will see eagles circling in the sky, climbing higher and higher as they ride these rising columns of air. Eagles also soar by using winds, called updrafts, that hit mountain ranges and are forced upward.

Unfortunately, eagles cannot depend on thermals and updrafts all the time. Since the ground gets heated unevenly depending on how the sun strikes the different surfaces, thermals are spaced irregularly across the landscape. Updrafts can be spotty, too—they do not occur over the prairies or the sea. So while eagles are soaring they often have to switch to other kinds of flight.

Eagles use gliding flight to move between thermals. Holding

their wings back just a little allows them to cruise along without flapping. If there are no updrafts to hold them up, gliding eagles slowly lose altitude. But as they approach the next thermal, they open their wings again and ride the rising air high above the earth.

The bateleur, the snake eagle that hunts the African grasslands, is designed for fast gliding. In fact, its long, narrow wings and very small tail prevent it from gliding slowly; its slowest cruising speeds are between 35 and 50 mph (56 and 80 kph). Most eagles usually cruise at only about 20 to 40 mph (32 to 64 kph).

While hunting, some eagles can go into a steep dive called a stoop. From a soaring or gliding position, they tuck their wings down and back, plummeting like a missile at maximum speeds of up to 150 to 200 mph (241 to 322 kph). This allows them to attack prey quickly and powerfully with striking feet or slashing talons, often killing a duck in midair or a squirrel on the ground. Then they open their wings quickly to pull out of the dive. Falcons are famous for stooping, but many eagles, like the golden eagle, do it as well.

Another kind of bird flight, hovering, is uncommon among eagles. Hovering involves flapping the wings in a short arc with the body tilted upward and the tail fanned out and at a sharp angle to the ground. It is a way of perching in the air in areas where there are no solid perches available, as in grassland or tundra. European snake eagles sometimes hover while hunting their prey in these treeless landscapes.

What Do Eagles Eat?

As we have seen, almost everything about eagles is designed for hunting. Their wings carry them swiftly and easily to prey. They kill quickly and neatly with their feet and talons. Their beaks tear

FISH IS ONE OF THE MAIN FOODS EATEN BY BALD EAGLES.

apart food into bite-sized chunks, which their bodies digest and use efficiently.

The different species in the eagle family eat a wide range of food—large insects, fish, snakes, lizards, birds, squirrels, rabbits, monkeys, and even small deer or antelope. The larger the eagle, the bigger the prey. The small Ayres' hawk-eagle weaves in and out of branches to catch the small birds it eats, while the large crowned eagle regularly eats small antelopes and monkeys.

Different methods of hunting are also determined by the kind of habitat an eagle's prey occupies. Many eagles, such as snake eagles, prey on animals that live in forests or along forest edges, so they prefer to spend most of their time hunting from perches. A perch in a good hunting area offers a place to sit and watch and blend into the surroundings. Once a snake eagle spots its prey it can pounce down quickly, weaving around brush to cover its attack.

Golden eagles, on the other hand, soar over a large area and then glide down or stoop onto a jackrabbit or a ground squirrel. These prey animals have a much larger range than snakes, so the golden eagle has adapted its own range to the

COMPETITION FOR FOOD IS OFTEN VERY FIERCE, EVEN BETWEEN EAGLES OF THE SAME SPECIES, LIKE THESE GOLDEN EAGLES.

range of its prey. The Indian black eagle is adapted to soar very slowly over treetops, looking for birds' nests and the eggs inside, one of its main foods; it also has a special straight talon on its hind toe, useful for piercing the eggs. Soaring is less work than flapping from perch to perch, but soaring eagles and their shadows are more visible to their prey.

Fish eagles, like Steller's sea-eagle, skim low over the water as they hunt. They snatch fish out of the water with one foot and hardly get wet. The African fish eagle hunts catfish, which surface often for air. The white-bellied sea-eagle hunts one of the most venomous snakes in the world, the sea snake.

Some grassland species, like the greater spotted eagle, will be drawn to the smoke of wildfires. They soar over the fire front, waiting for small animals trying to escape the blaze. Some species even hunt on foot, like the lesser spotted eagle, which struts around on its long legs grabbing up small mammals, lizards, and insects. Most eagles are solitary hunters, but crowned eagles of Africa sometimes work in pairs. One pursues a monkey, for example, sending it into the trees, while the other comes at it from the other side, leaving the monkey nowhere to run.

All eagles are meat eaters and mostly catch live prey, but some eagles also feed on carrion, or the flesh of dead animals. Eating found meat makes sense because eagles do not have to waste energy catching it. It is also easier to steal food. Some eagles chase other birds and pirate food from them. Bald eagles are famous for stealing food from ospreys, another fish-eating raptor. Golden eagles, bateleurs, white-bellied sea-eagles, brown snake eagles, and the tawny eagle also pirate food.

With all their great tools for catching and killing, you would think eagles were very successful at what they do. But actually, more often than not, they fail to catch their prey. That's why they spend so much time trying and why they take food from other

THE LARGE NUMBERS OF SALMON THAT SWIM UPRIVER DURING SPAWNING SEASON ARE A FOOD SOURCE TAKEN ADVANTAGE OF BY MANY DIFFERENT PREDATORS, INCLUDING THIS BALD EAGLE AND BROWN BEAR IN MIKVIK CREEK, ALASKA.

birds or eat found meat when they can. And food is not always available year-round in some eagles' territories. When food becomes sparse, many eagles fly to their second home.

Two Homes

Many birds have more than one home. They have breeding ranges and nonbreeding ranges, sometimes called summer and

winter ranges. Many people think birds leave their summer ranges to escape winter cold, but scientists think birds migrate to take advantage of seasonal food sources. Raptors that summer in the north would not have much to eat when winter snows cover the ground, sending much of their prey into hibernation. Migration allows them to stay active year-round. Eagles in areas with mild climates all year, like the white-tailed eagle and the Spanish eagle in southern Europe, usually stay put because they have food available in one location all year long.

Breeding ranges include both a nesting range and a hunting range. These can be the same or nearly the same size, but more often the nesting area is only a small part of the hunting range. The nonbreeding range is used only as a hunting range. Most eagles that migrate will spend more time in the breeding range. Not every species and not every bird in every species migrates. Most raptors are only partial migrants, which means that only part of their populations travels from home to home.

Eagles and other raptors travel by day and over land for their migrations, even if this means taking a long detour around a lake or bay. This is because they need to take advantage of mountain updrafts and thermals, which occur only during daytime hours and over land. Cold fronts from the north tell birds that it is time to head south in the fall and provide the right winds to get them on their way. Warm fronts from the south in the spring send the birds north.

Eagles' seasonal movements can be over a very short distance, or the eagles can travel for hundreds or even thousands of miles every year. Some golden eagles travel only from higher elevation areas to lower elevation areas in the same region, while others travel from Canada to the southern United States. Geography usually determines the travel route. In the United States, birds follow the mountain chains, rivers, and coastlines, which tend to run north-south. In Europe these features run more east-west. Raptors eventually get crowded together as they cross the narrow land bridges. These locations—around Veracruz in Mexico and Eilat in Israel, for example—are the best places to see migrating birds. Sometimes birders see thousands in a single day.

Though it seems to be essential for the survival of most eagles, migration has its costs. It is usually a long and very hazardous trip; most eagles that migrate long distances eat very little or not at all during migration. They depend upon stored-up energy. Of all the birds that migrate (not just eagles), only slightly more than half will make it back to their breeding ranges the next spring. They die along the way or in their winter homes. It is easy to get blown off course, starve along the way, or be caught by a predator.

6

The Life Cycle

Much of a mating eagle pair's year is taken up with the various duties and rituals of the breeding cycle, the period from courtship to dispersal, when young eagles leave their parents' care. Breeding differs from species to species. Some eagles need to breed in a very specific location. Others are less picky about where they put their nests as long as the site provides good protection from predators and a food source is nearby.

Eagles usually mate once a year. The fledging period, or time between hatching and the young bird's first flight, averages eighty to ninety days in eagles. A few species, like the crowned eagle of Africa and the harpy eagle of South America, mate only every other year with a breeding cycle of up to 500 days. They provide food for their young for as long as eleven months after they first leave the nest. This might be because the parents want to make sure their young are strong when they leave their care.

THE ADULT BALD EAGLE PICKS APART THE KILL AND FEEDS IT PIECE BY PIECE TO THE EAGLET UNTIL IT CAN LEARN TO EAT FOR ITSELF.

Courtship

Mating starts with courtship, which in some cases can be very active. Some male birds, like the golden eagle, do a lot of soaring and diving to impress their mates. Others, like the bald eagle, are more aggressive. The male and the female will soar together and then the male will dive at the female. She will then turn upside-down and the birds will grasp and lock their talons together, holding their wings back out of the way as they fall somersaulting hundreds of feet down through the sky.

Each species has its own individual courtship rituals. While these often involve some kind of flight display, eagles have a variety of ways to get the attention of a prospective mate. Sometimes during courtship, males will bring females food, which may serve to save her strength for egg laying. The males continue to bring food throughout the incubation and fledging periods. The goal of this courting for both the male and female eagle is to make sure that each bird secures a mate that is strong and fit and capable of raising healthy offspring that have a good chance of survival.

Eagles are usually monogamous, meaning they have only one mate until death. One unusual case is the bateleur, the African snake eagle. Males of this species will mate with more than one female, a practice called polygyny, which is more typical of mammals.

Nest Building

After courtship the eagles concentrate on building their nest. Most eagle nests are made of sticks and branches, which are gathered from living trees rather than from the ground, where branches are more likely to be dried out or rotted. The nests are usually built in trees across a few strong branches or on cliffs.

Golden eagles build their nests in many different places—cliffs, trees, sometimes even in abandoned buildings. They may also build as many as ten different "backup" nests in case the one they are using is destroyed. The bald eagle, like many eagles, will use its nest year after year; it may even pass it on to its young. A nest may be used for up to thirty-five years. The nests are added to every year; after many years the nest may be a great pile of sticks as large as 10 feet (3 m) across and 20 feet (6 m) deep.

A CLIFF NEST PROVIDES THIS NEWLY HATCHED GOLDEN EAGLET EXCELLENT PROTECTION FROM PREDATORS.

One bald eagle nest was used for thirty years and weighed two tons (1.8 metric tons) —as much as a car!

Some eagles defend their nests vigorously and noisily, and will strike intruders—even considerably larger intruders like human scientists. Other eagles are easily scared off their nests, and they may abandon them, leaving the chicks to die. It is very important for people to be careful around nests and avoid going near them during nesting season.

Mating

Eagles mate over several weeks to make sure the eggs are fertilized. The male will perch on the female's back—he may have to curl his toes so his talons do not hurt her. He moves his tail to one side as the female raises hers, and their cloacas touch. This allows the male's sperm to enter the female and, with luck, fertilize an ovum, or egg. (The genitalia, or sex organs, are inside the bird. They are tiny most of the year but grow very large at breeding time.)

Once the ovum, which is actually an egg yolk, is fertilized, it travels down the oviduct, gathering everything it will need— the white of the egg, used for moisture; the shell membranes; and then the hard shell for protection. The passage of the egg through the oviduct takes about twenty-four hours. A female eagle lays an average of two eggs per clutch, two to three days apart. Then she sits and waits.

Raising Young

Eggs. Depending on the species, eagle eggs hatch in forty to fifty days. During this time the female is almost always brooding, or sitting on the eggs to keep them warm; the male sometimes takes her place during the day if she is off stretching her wings. The female is better adapted to brood than the male. She has a special brood patch that covers the eggs. This is a featherless area of skin on her belly with a dense concentration of blood vessels that keep the area warmer than the rest of her body. The eggs need to be kept at a fairly precise temperature, ideally between 98 degrees Fahrenheit and 100 degrees Fahrenheit (36.7 to 37.8° C). If the eggs are warmer than 103 degrees Fahrenheit (39.5° C) or colder than 95 degrees Fahrenheit (35° C), they may fail to hatch.

In cold climates, the eagles may need to sit on the eggs almost constantly. In warmer parts of the world, eagles may leave the nest for short periods because there is less danger of the eggs losing heat. Instead they may have to block the sun with their bodies so the eggs don't get too hot. The eggs also need to be turned occasionally so the embryo doesn't stick to the shell.

When the young birds are ready to come out of the egg, they start pecking from the inside with a small nub on the tip of their beaks called an egg tooth. (It will fall off as the chick starts to grow.) It may take a full day for the baby eagles, or eaglets, to break their way out of the shell.

Eaglets. When the eaglets first come into the world, they are mostly helpless: they can barely move, and they are blind. They have a patchy layer of downy feathers on their bodies, but they cannot keep themselves warm. They will still need to be brooded for a couple of weeks until they grow their next layer of down.

Young eagle chicks are all beak and feet—they need these right away for eating. While the other parts of their bodies are still very small, the eagle's beak and feet—hunting tools in wait-ing—grow quickly, reaching maturity while the chick is only half

A NEWLY HATCHED BALD EAGLET CAN HARDLY MOVE AND IS BLIND.

its adult size. It takes lots of eating for the eagle's body to catch up to its beak. The chicks do not eat for the first day or two, but once they start, feeding and sleeping are all they do for the next few weeks. The mother eagle tears off small bits of meat from an animal that the father has brought and feeds them to each chick. Until the chicks get a little bigger and the mother can leave the nest, the male does most of the hunting and also plucks the feathers and removes the head from each kill. This makes it easier for the chicks to be fed and it helps keep the nest clean.

The competition for food is fierce, and the younger eagle, the one hatched second, usually dies of starvation or is killed by its older sibling. (If there is a lot of food available, however, both chicks usually survive.) Scientists think this happens because it gives the firstborn bird a better chance of survival. Also, laying two eggs has its advantages; if something happens to one egg, there will still be a chick to raise. Regular feeding allows the remaining chick to grow very quickly. Bald eagles bring food to their chicks four or five times a day.

About one-third of the way through the fledging period, the young eagle's first feathers start growing in. These are usually the wing or tail feathers, both important for flying. The bird can usually stand and walk now. Once the chick is fully feathered, the parents come around only to bring food. The young bird can keep itself warm and feed from the kills the parents bring. Instead of begging, it now adopts the threat posture—raising its wings and covering its food—that adults use when feeding. It spends its time between feedings watching insects and animals or playing with sticks.

On Their Own

Soon the young eagle is ready to leave the nest. In the days before it is ready to try its first flight, it will flap its wings a lot, testing them out. It might hop along on a branch near the nest, getting its bearings. Then one day the eagle will lift its wings and suddenly drop from the limb, flapping hard, then glide across a clearing and land awkwardly on a tree branch. It might not be the most graceful of flights, but the young eagle will get better fast. If it is a golden eagle, in just two weeks it will be soaring high above the mountains.

The ability to fly is only a step toward independence. In some eagle species, the parents may continue to feed their young for almost a year. This time, between a young eagle's first flight and its departure from its parents, is called the post-fledging period. This extended stay around the nest gives young eagles time to

THIS SEVEN-WEEK-OLD BALD EAGLE IS ADOPTING A THREAT POSTURE, IN DEFENSE OF ITSELF OR ITS FOOD.

practice hunting and flying. Eventually they will leave to find their own hunting territory or, if they are a migratory species, to head south for the coming winter—if they survive, that is. Many eagles—around 50 to 80 percent, depending on the species—do not survive their first year, and 90 percent of young bald eagles born in any given year do not make it to adulthood. Most die of starvation; competition is fierce and food is not always reliable or plentiful. Those that do live through their first year still face many obstacles to survival.

This immature bald eagle is getting ready to take its first flight.

7 The Fate of Eagles

Threats to Eagles

Eagles the world over are fighting for survival, and some are barely hanging on. As we have seen, it is not easy being an eagle. In the best of conditions, many young eagles die of natural causes. Those that live through the challenges of their first year learn to take advantage of every available food source—from insects to antelope to carrion—to help them survive. Some eagles even thrive, living long and well on the strength of their instinctive hunting skills.

Still, even as individuals flourish, the long-term survival of many eagle species is not assured. As the human population grows and people turn more and more wild areas into human settlements, it is getting harder for eagles to find the habitat and the food they need to stay alive. Add to that a host of other threats, from hunting to chemical poisoning, and it becomes clear that eagles face many difficult challenges to survival.

BALD EAGLES ARE EASY TO IDENTIFY AS THEY SOAR OVERHEAD. THE BACK-LIGHTING ON THIS EAGLE SHOWS OFF ITS BOLD WHITE TAIL.

Hunting and Sport Killing. Human hunters are a serious threat to eagle survival. For centuries people all over the world have thought of eagles and other raptors as pests, competitors for game, and destroyers of livestock. They have responded by killing raptors. In the United States, shooting raptors was a common practice throughout the nineteenth century and well into the twentieth century. Many men gathered on high hilltops and mountains during the birds' migration and shot raptors all day as they passed overhead. The bodies piled up on the hillsides. Since these times, research has shown that raptors are not the villains humankind has made them out to be. They are responsible for only a very small number of livestock deaths and mostly feed on dead animals or stillborn young.

Though raptor hunting has been curbed in the United States, it has not been stopped. More bald eagles die of bullet wounds than of anything else. Some people will even shoot endangered birds for fun, despite federal and international laws that protect them. In southern Europe about 100,000 raptors are shot every year as they cross the Mediterranean Sea in great numbers on their migration route. Hunters line up along the shores to kill these magnificent creatures just because they are easy targets.

Eagles can also die from eating poisoned carrion. Game animals wounded by lead shot sometimes escape hunters but still die. Eagles feeding on these dead animals can eat the lead shot, which slowly poisons them. They become so weak they cannot fly or feed themselves, and die from the effects. Eagles can also be lured by carrion to deadly leg-hold traps or poisoned bait that hunters set out for them and other predators.

The collection and use of feathers and other eagle parts for Native American ceremonies is another threat to eagle survival—one that illustrates that the issue of wildlife protection can have

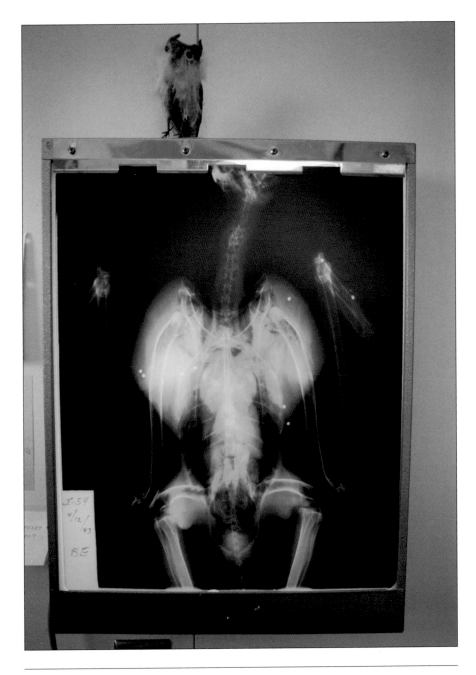

In this X-ray, lead pellets can be seen as bright dots inside the body and wings of this bald eagle. Shooting is the leading cause of death of bald eagles.

Native Americans used eagle feathers for many purposes, including ceremonial items such as this war bonnet worn by Plains Indians.

more than one side. Possession of eagles, their feathers, or other body parts is a violation of federal law. But the United States' Bald and Golden Eagle Protection Act recognizes the right of Native Americans to practice traditional ceremonies and allows their limited use of eagle parts. The National Eagle Repository in Denver, Colorado, provides eagles (ones that are found dead) and eagle parts to federally recognized tribes. Molted feathers from eagles in wildlife rehabilitation centers and zoos are also used. A long waiting list exists because the number of dead eagles found every year does not meet the demand for them. This has led to a black market in eagles, which are illegally killed and sold, mostly to Native Americans for use in rituals, dances, and powwows.

Some Native American cultures are fighting this law, seeking exemptions so they can continue to practice the traditional ceremonies that help keep their culture alive. Other tribal members do not believe that eagles should be killed or tortured for their ceremonies. They say that Indians have long worshipped and respected the eagles and do not need to kill them for their feathers.

DDT and Other Chemicals. Many raptors suffer poisoning from pesticides and herbicides, the chemicals sprayed on crops to kill bugs and weeds. Since their development after World War II, pesticides have been widely used by farmers all over the world. Raptor species like bald eagles, ospreys, and peregrine falcons have been especially affected because they feed on animals that have been poisoned by pesticides. As insects that feed on crops sprayed with pesticides are in turn fed upon by birds and fish, the chemicals become more concentrated in the bodies of the insect eaters. When raptors prey on these poisoned animals, the already high concentrations become higher still. Over time a female bald eagle feeding on pesticide-ridden trout gets

DESPITE LAWS REGULATING PESTICIDE USE, MANY BIRDS STILL DIE AS A RESULT OF POISONING BY THESE AGRICULTURAL CHEMICALS. THESE BALD EAGLES WERE FOUND DEAD FROM POISONING IN A FARM FIELD IN VIRGINIA.

a very high dose of poison. She may not die, but the poison causes her eggs' shells to be so thin that the brooding mother's weight crushes them.

Pesticide use in the thirty years following World War II caused many populations of raptors to drop precipitously, bringing them close to extinction. As a result, many of the chemicals that sickened birds were outlawed in the United States in the 1970s. Unfortunately, pesticides stay in the environment a long time, so some birds are still having problems. Also, many tropical countries have not outlawed these pesticides and are still using them. Birds become contaminated during their winter stay in their southern ranges in these parts of the world. Dangerous chemicals are still being used even in the United States. In the late 1980s, about 2.4 million birds were killed by a commonly used pesticide called carbofuran.

Habitat Destruction. The natural landscape is often dramatically changed by human activity. Cutting down trees for wood products, clearing land for agriculture, building superhighways— all these activities alter and sometimes destroy wildlife habitat. In fact, one-third of the world's wildlands have been changed by human use, reducing the amount of available habitat for both the eagles and their prey. Tropical forests in developing countries in South America and Africa are especially vulnerable, with millions of acres cut down every year.

The problem is even more drastic for eagles that need large areas of unbroken, mature forests to survive, like the harpy eagle and the Philippine eagle. As their habitats are destroyed or changed, these eagles will be crowded into smaller and smaller territories, competing among themselves for less and less food and fewer nesting areas. As logging companies build more and more roads to get to the trees, the forest becomes accessible to people who come to kill or capture raptors and other wildlife for food, sport, or the pet trade. If these trends continue without laws and enforcement to stop them, many eagle species will eventually become extinct.

MANY WILD EAGLES ARE CAUGHT FOR THE FALCONRY AND PET TRADE. THIS BIRD BEING TIED UP AT THIS REFUGEE CAMP IN DASHT-I-QALA, AFGHANISTAN, WAS TO BE SOLD TO AN AMATEUR FALCONER IN A GULF ARAB COUNTRY. LAWS IN THE UNITED STATES PROHIBIT THE CAPTURING OR HARMING OF WILD RAPTORS. ONLY CAPTIVE-BRED BIRDS OR WILD ONES THAT HAVE BEEN INJURED AND CANNOT BE RETURNED TO THE WILD CAN BE USED FOR THIS PURPOSE.

And it is not only eagles' summer and winter habitats that are being destroyed. Areas that eagles use as stopovers on their migration routes are in danger, too. In Veracruz, Mexico, for example, where many birds stop on their long journey, the tropical forest is being cut down and turned into pasture for livestock and fields for sugarcane.

Protection of Endangered Eagles

Legal Protection. The law is one way to protect eagles and their habitats. In response to the hunting and killing of huge numbers of birds, the United States and other countries have passed laws to protect them. And this has helped many populations of eagles, like the bald eagle, to become healthy again. But laws are not always enough. Many countries do not have the money to pay people to enforce wildlife protection laws, and many people disobey them.

Education and Habitat Protection. In response to declining populations of eagles, many organizations have been formed to protect them and their habitat. Organizations do this in a number of ways, from working for strong international laws to buying and preserving land for eagle habitat. Of all the work conservation organizations do, education may be the most important. Species extinction and habitat loss are greatest in countries where laws and governments are not doing anything to protect eagles and other animals. When it comes to a choice between saving an endangered eagle and feeding your children, most people would, of course, choose to take care of their families. Many organizations are finding ways to work with local communities to teach them ways to feed their families and make a living while protecting habitat. They teach farming or fishing practices that do not destroy natural resources. They may also suggest to poor farmers and fishermen that taking care of their land, waters, and wildlife can make their home a place tourists want to visit, and tourism can strengthen the local economy.

Healing the Sick. Many organizations work to help injured birds and animals. These wildlife rehabilitation centers have staff trained in veterinary medicine, and they provide safe, comfortable enclosures where the animals can heal. Many of these centers focus on birds of prey. Their main mission is to try to heal the birds and return them to the wild. Some birds do fully heal, but others are too badly injured to fly or catch their own food. The permanently injured birds are often kept and cared for, and some are trained to become educators, visiting schools with their handlers to teach young people about raptors. Others are

THIS RECENTLY HATCHED BALD EAGLET WAS HAND-FED AT THE PATUXENT WILDLIFE RESEARCH CENTER IN LAUREL, MARYLAND. IT AND OTHERS LIKE IT HAVE BEEN RAISED BY HUMANS TO HELP THE WILD POPULATION OF THIS ONCE ENDANGERED EAGLE RECOVER.

kept on display so visitors can watch these survivors in their enclosures; this helps people learn how healthy raptors live in the wild and why it is so important to protect them. Many wildlife rehabilitation centers offer public education programs and raptor demonstrations. Some centers also have programs in which they raise birds for reintroduction to the wild.

Management. Governments and conservation organizations help species in danger of extinction with a variety of programs aimed at boosting their populations. Often eagles are reintroduced into their former habitats, but it is not always an easy task. Many adult eagles cannot be moved from place to place because they have a very strong homing instinct. By releasing young birds, reintroduction programs take advantage of fledged eagles' natural desire to disperse and find their own territories.

Another population-boosting technique is called captive breeding, but this also does not always work with eagles. Most eagle species cannot be bred in captivity because their courtship displays require more space than zoos and other such sites can provide. Also, birds imprint on the first large animal they see, so eagle chicks might think the humans caring for them are their parents and would not be able to learn how to survive in the wild. Sometimes humans do raise eagle chicks, feeding them with a hand puppet that looks like an eagle so they won't imprint on people.

Another way to reintroduce eagles to the wild is with a technique called hacking. Chicks are taken from nests in the wild and raised by humans in locations where the species has died out. They are put into a nest box in the appropriate habitat for the species. The birds can see the area around them but not the humans who feed them. After they learn to fly and start to hunt for themselves, the humans leave food for them for a few weeks. Soon the birds disperse and scout out their own territories.

One of the best ways to raise eagle chicks is called double-clutching. In this method, eggs are taken from one nesting pair of eagles and given to another pair that are unable to have their own chicks—usually because these parents lay only infertile eggs or because their eggs are contaminated with pesticides. The first pair of eagles will mate again and lay more eggs to

Endangered harpy eagles, like this one at the World Center for Birds of Prey in Panama, are being bred in captivity in order to bolster the wild population.

replace the missing ones. The infertile eggs of the second pair are replaced with the fertile eggs, and these eagles act as adoptive parents to the chicks, raising them as if they were their own. This increases the overall number of chicks raised. Double-clutching is one of the ways the bald eagle was saved from near extinction.

Artificial nests can help save endangered species, too. In areas where there aren't many good trees for nesting, poles or platforms are set up to encourage eagles to nest. Sometimes nesting platforms are more than simply helpful; they can save birds' lives. In the western United States, golden eagles sometimes nest on electrical transmission towers because there aren't many trees. Their wingspans are so wide that when the eagles perch on a tower the tip of each of their wings can touch a different wire, completing an electrical current that kills them. Utility companies now put up platforms on safe parts of the towers, and eagles use them as nest sites.

Endangered Eagles

While there is much more positive attention paid these days to wildlife and the dangers of extinction than ever before, many animals and many eagles in particular are still critically endangered.

Philippine Eagle. The Philippine eagle is considered one of the most endangered birds in the world; scientists estimate that there are fewer than one hundred left in the wild. This eagle lives on the Philippine Islands in the South Pacific Ocean. It formerly lived on many islands in the Philippine chain, but human overpopulation, habitat destruction, and poaching for the illegal pet trade have reduced its range to only two islands. The Peregrine Fund and the Philippine Eagle Foundation have successfully bred Philippine eagles in captivity with the hopes of returning them to the wild. Programs to help local communities protect these magnificent birds are also under way, but the population numbers are still dropping, and much more needs to be done to save the Philippine eagle.

Madagascar Fish Eagle. The rapid development of Madagascar, an island nation east of Africa, has quickly reduced habitat for the Madagascar fish eagle. As a coastal species, the fish eagle competes directly for resources—fish and territory—with people. It has been known to steal fish from fishing nets. Its habits of soaring and perching atop tall trees and its lack of fear of humans has made it an easy target for hunters. The Madagascar fish eagle's numbers are very low. Fewer than one hundred were living in the wild according to late-1980s field surveys, making it one of the rarest raptors in the world.

Spanish Imperial Eagle. Only about 110 to 160 pairs of Spanish eagles are left in the wild in central and southern Spain. Soon after this eagle was first discovered in 1860, its numbers declined quickly because of shooting and egg-poaching. Recently, double-clutching has helped increase its numbers, but many eagles still die from electrocution by power lines, lack of food (their main prey, rabbits, are dying from disease), and poisoning by shooting clubs whose members say the birds are competing for their game animals.

Bald Eagle. The bald eagle is a success story of effective legislation, habitat protection, and reintroduction. Its populations have rebounded in recent years to a level that allowed the federal government to adjust the bird's status from "endangered" to "threatened" in 1995. But this was after decades of very low population levels caused by hunting, habitat destruction, and pesticide poisoning.

Hacking programs enabled young bald eagles from western Canada and Alaska to be raised and released in many parts of their range. While their numbers today are nowhere near

THE PHILIPPINE HAWK-EAGLE IS LOSING HABITAT AT AN ALARMING PACE. HUNTING
AND THE CUTTING OF FORESTS ARE MAKING THIS ALREADY SCARCE BIRD EVEN RARER.

numbers before 1800, when there were between 25,000 and 75,000 wild bald eagles, populations have grown steadily over the last twenty-five years, from 407 territorial pairs in 1976 to more than 4,000 in 1993. The numbers of wintering bald eagles in the United States has also risen dramatically, from 2,772 in 1968 to 13,807 in 1983.

Eagles have always inspired both admiration and fear in humans. As a result, eagles have earned a place in our religions and our cultures, as icons and symbols, and also as targets of anger and mistrust. But more recently, we have begun to learn the importance of these birds, not only to us, but to all of nature. As predators, they play key roles in many different ecosystems all over the world and are inextricably linked to many other animal populations.

In the United States, we were fortunate to have recognized the importance of bald eagles and their right to exist before we lost them forever. Let's hope this success story and others can inspire people all over the world to protect the animals and their habitats that humans have helped to put at risk.

Glossary

aerodynamic—the quality of a surface that is rounded or streamlined to reduce wind drag, thereby allowing for faster speeds, as when an eagle pulls in its wings and flattens all of its feathers to allow for quick glides or stoops

barb—one of the many small, thin parts that make up the vane of the feather

barbule—tiny hooklike parts that hold the barbs together; they allow a bird to "zip" its feathers closed so they are smooth, aerodynamic, and water repellent

breed—to give birth or hatch

breeding cycle—the entire process of reproduction in eagles, including courtship, mating, nest building, incubation, fledging, and post-fledging

brood—to sit on and hatch eggs; to keep young warm by sitting on or next to them

brood patch—a patch of bare flesh with extra blood vessels on the underside of female birds that is used to keep eggs and chicks warm

captive breeding—hatching baby birds or raising other young animals in a zoo or other location that is not the animal's natural habitat

carnivorous—meat eating

carrion—the meat of dead animals

cere—area of bare skin between an eagle's eyes and its beak; helps to keep the area around the eyes and mouth clean

cloaca—the opening beneath the tail on a bird's body inside which are the intestinal, genital, and urinary tracts

crop—a pouch in a bird's throat where food is stored before its slow release into the stomach

dispersal—the time when a young bird leaves its parents' care and seeks out its own territory

double-clutching—inducing a bird to lay a second set, or clutch, of eggs by removing the first set from the nest; this method is used to increase numbers of a population, such as the bald eagle or the endangered Spanish Imperial eagle

egg tooth—the small bony knob on a newborn chick's bill used to break open the eggshell at hatching

fledging period—the early time of a bird's life, from hatching to first flight

gizzard—a muscular pouch behind a bird's stomach that helps break down food for digestion

habitat—the type of environment where an animal lives; for example, a grassland or a desert

hacking—raising young birds in an enclosure or box in their natural habitat; the humans remain unseen during this time to avoid imprinting

hatchling—a newly hatched bird; a chick

imprinting—when a young bird or other animal first sees and bonds with its parent; a hatchling may also imprint on the first large animal or person it sees

keratin—a tough, skinlike substance of which hair, bones, fingernails, hooves, beaks, and talons are made

migrate—to move from one home to another on a regular, usually seasonal, basis to take advantage of food sources; some eagles migrate long distances, such as from North America to South America

mob—to aggressively drive away a predator, as when flocks of crows chase eagles or hawks away from their territory

molt—to shed old feathers and grow new ones; an immature eagle molts many times before getting its adult plumage; an adult eagle may molt annually or biannually

monogamy—the practice of a male and female mating for life

ornithologist—a scientist who studies birds

pellet—in birds, a regurgitated plug made up of undigested bones, fur, hair, and feathers

pirating—stealing food from another bird, as when a bald eagle steals food from an osprey

polygyny—the practice of a male mating with more than one female

predator—an animal that preys on other animals; a bird of prey

prey—animals that a predator hunts and eats

reproduction—the process of creating other organisms of the same kind

reverse sexual dimorphism—the condition in which the females of a given species or animal group are larger than the males; in most terrestrial vertebrates, the males are larger than the females

savanna—a flat grassland of tropical or subtropical regions

spicules—hardened, pointed scales on the bottoms of the feet of fish eagles; these help the eagles grasp slippery fish

stoop—a headfirst dive used by some species of eagles, such as golden eagles, and other raptors to kill or knock prey out of the sky or to attack them on the ground or in the water

talons—sharp nails like claws on the tips of the toes of raptors used for catching and killing prey

vane—the soft, flexible part around the central shaft of a feather; this includes the barbs and barbules

Species Checklist

This is a complete list of all the eagles in the world: sixty-four species in twenty-two genera (groups of closely related species) in four groups.

Genus	Common Name	Scientific species name
Booted Eagles		
Aquila	Golden eagle	*A. chrysaetos*
	Greater spotted eagle	*A. clanga*
	Gurney's eagle	*A. gurneyi*
	Imperial eagle	*A. heliaca*
	Lesser spotted eagle	*A. pomarina*
	Spanish Imperial eagle	*A. adalberti*
	Steppe eagle	*A. nipalensis*
	Tawny eagle	*A. rapax*
	Verreaux's eagle	*A. verreuaxii*
	Wahlberg's eagle	*A. whalbergi*
	Wedge-tailed eagle	*A. audax*
Hieraaetu	African hawk-eagle	*H. spilogaster*
	Ayres' hawk-eagle	*H. ayresii*
	Bonelli's eagle	*H. fasciatus*
	Booted eagle	*H. pennatus*
	Little eagle	*H. morphnoides*
	Rufous-bellied eagle	*H. kienerii*
Ictinaetus	Indian black eagle	*I. malayensis*
Lophaetus	Long-crested eagle	*L. occipitalis*
Oroaetus	Black-and-chestnut eagle	*O. isidori*
Polemaetus	Martial eagle	*P. bellicosus*

Spizaetus	Black hawk-eagle	*S. tyrannus*
	Blyth's hawk-eagle	*S. alboniger*
	Cassin's hawk-eagle	*S. africanus*
	Changeable hawk-eagle	*S. cirrhatus*
	Javan hawk-eagle	*S. bartelsi*
	Mountain hawk-eagle	*S. nipalensis*
	Ornate hawk-eagle	*S. ornatus*
	Philippine hawk-eagle	*S. philippensis*
	Sulawesi hawk-eagle	*S. lanceolatus*
	Wallace's hawk-eagle	*S. nanus*
Spizastur	Black-and-white hawk-eagle	*S. melanoleucus*
Stephanoaetus	Crowned hawk-eagle	*S. coronatus*

Fish and Sea Eagles

Gypohierax	Vulturine fish eagle	*G. angolensis*
Haliaeetus	African fish eagle	*H. vocifer*
	Bald eagle	*H. leucocephalus*
	Madagascar fish eagle	*H. vociferoides*
	Pallas's fish eagle	*H. leucoryphus*
	Sanfords's sea-eagle	*H. sanfordi*
	Steller's sea-eagle	*H. pelagicus*
	White-bellied sea-eagle	*H. leucogaster*
	White-tailed eagle	*H. albicilla*
Ichthyophaga	Gray-headed fish eagle	*I. ichthyaetus*
	Lesser fish eagle	*I. humilis*

Harpy Eagles

Harpia	Harpy eagle	*H. harpyja*
Harpyhaliaetus	(Black) Solitary eagle	*H. solitarious*
	Crowned (solitary) eagle	*H. coronatus*

Harpyopsis	New Guinea eagle	*H. novaeguineae*
Morphnus	Guiana crested eagle	*M. guianensis*
Pithecophaga	Philippine (monkey-eating) eagle	*P. jefferyi*

Snake and Serpent Eagles

Circaetus	Banded snake eagle	*C. cinerascens*
	Black-chested snake eagle	*C. pectoralis*
	Brown snake eagle	*C. cinereus*
	Fasciated snake eagle	*C. fasciolatus*
	Short-toed eagle	*C. gallicus*
Dryotriorchis	Congo serpent eagle	*D. spectabilis*
Eutriorchis	Madagascar serpent eagle	*E. astur*
Spilornis	Andaman serpent eagle	*S. elgini*
	Crested serpent eagle	*S. cheela*
	Mountain serpent eagle	*S. kinabaluensis*
	Nicobar serpent eagle	*S. minimus*
	Philippine serpent eagle	*S. holospilus*
	Sulawesi serpent eagle	*S. rufipectus*
Terathopius	Bateleur	*T. ecaudatus*

Further Research

Books and Magazines

Eliot, John L. "Bald Eagles Come Back from the Brink." *National Geographic*, July 2002.

Pasquier, Roger F. *Watching Birds: An Introduction to Ornithology*. Houghton Mifflin Company, Boston, 1980.

Sattler, Helen Roney. *The Book of Eagles*. New York: Lothrop, Lee, and Shepard Books, William Morrow and Company, Inc., 1989.

Web Sites

http://www.eagles.org
  Dedicated to the protection and preservation of the American bald eagle; lots of useful links.

http://www.indiana.edu/~bradwood/eagles/native.htm
  Self-guided study of bald eagles including basic information on bald eagles and the human influence on them.

http://www.peregrinefund.org/index.html
  The site of the Peregrine Fund, an international organization that helps to protect birds of prey through captive breeding and conservation projects.

http://www.hawk-conservancy.org/prioreagles.shtml
  The Hawk Conservancy in England—photos and good species descriptions.

http://www.natureserve.org
  NatureServe is a leading source of information about rare and endangered species and threatened ecosystems.

http://www.raptor.cvm.umn.edu
  The Raptor Center of the University of Minnesota provides information on raptors and the center's rehabilitation efforts.

http://www.vinsweb.org/vrc/index.html
  The Vermont Raptor Center provides information on raptor rehabilitation and programs.

http://theraptortrust.org
  The Raptor Trust in Millington, New Jersey: good information on raptors, building nest boxes, and the resident raptors at the Trust.

Bibliography

Beans, Bruce E. *Eagle's Plume: Preserving the Life and Habitat of America's Bald Eagle*. New York: Scribner, 1996.

BirdLife International, Species Factsheet: Javan Hawk-eagle. http://www.birdlife.org.uk.

BirdLife International, Species Factsheet: Spanish Imperial eagle. http://www.birdlife.org.uk.

Brown, Leslie. *African Birds of Prey*. Boston: Houghton Mifflin Company, 1971.

Brown, Leslie. *The World of Animals: Eagles*. New York: Arco Publishing Co., Inc., 1970.

Brown, Leslie, and Dean Amadon. *Eagles, Hawks, and Falcons of the World*, vols. 1 and 2. New York: McGraw-Hill Book Co., 1968.

Dunne, Pete. *The Wind Masters: The Lives of North American Birds of Prey*. Boston: Houghton Mifflin Company, 1995.

Ehrlich, Paul R., David S. Dobkin, and Darryl Wheye. *The Birder's Handbook*. New York: Simon and Schuster, Inc., 1988.

Gerrard, Jon M. and Gary R. Bortolotti. *The Bald Eagle: Haunts and Habits of a Wilderness Monarch*. Washington, D.C.: Smithsonian Institution Press, 1988.

Gill, Frank B. *Ornithology*. New York: W. H. Freeman and Co., 1990.

Grossman, Mary L., and John Hamlet. *Birds of Prey of the World*. New York: Clarkson N. Potter, Inc., 1964.

Johnsgard, Paul A. *Hawks, Eagles, and Falcons of North America*. Washington, D.C.: Smithsonian Institution Press, 1990.

Proctor, Noble S., and Patrick J. Lynch. *Manual of Ornithology*. New Haven: Yale University Press, 1993.

Quammen, David. *The Song of the Dodo*. New York: Scribner, 1996.

Schueler, Donald G. *Incident at Eagle Ranch: Man and Predator in the American West*. San Francisco: Sierra Club Books, 1980.

Sutton, Clay, and Patricia Taylor Sutton. *How to Spot Hawks and Eagles*. Shelburne, Vermont: Chapters Publishing, Inc., 1996.

United States Fish and Wildlife Service. A Guide to the Laws and Treaties of the United States for Protecting Migratory Birds. http://migratorybirds.fws.gov/intrnltr/treatlaw.html

Weidensaul, Scott. *The Raptor Almanac*. New York: The Lyons Press, 2000.

Whitaker, Barbara. "On the Wings of Eagles, the Fate of a California Island." *New York Times*, July 29, 2002. http://www.nytimes.com/2002/07/29/science/29EAGL.html

Williams, Ted. "Golden Eagles for the Gods." *Audubon*, March–April, 2001, 30–39.

World Wildlife Fund. Species Under Threat: Madagascar Fish-eagle. http://www.panda.org

World Wildlife Fund. Species Under Threat: Philippine Eagle. http://www.panda.org

Index

Page numbers in **boldface** are illustrations and charts.

maps
  breeding ranges, 34

adaptations, 10, 42–45, 50, 52–56, 64–71
aerodynamics, 60, 64–66
anatomy, **52**, 52–56, **57**, 58

bald eagles, 8–10, **9**, 15–16, **19**, **31**, 33, **34**, **40**, **53**, **55**, 62, **62**, **68**, 70, **71**, **72**, **75**, 76, 77, **82**, **83**, **85**, **90**, 97, 98, 100, 105
bateleurs, 46–49, **48**, 67, 70, 76, 106
beaks (or bills), 30, 38, **41**, 42, 45, **53**, 53–54, 79–80
booted eagles, 20, 33, 35–38, **35**, 55, 104
breeding, 95–97, **96**
breeding ranges, **34**, 71–72
brooding, 78–79, 90

calls, 37–38, **39**, 44
captivity, 18, **92**, 95
ceres, **41**, 46, 53–54
classification, 30, 32, 38, 42, 45, 104–106
color, 10, 33, 36, 37, 38, 41, 44, 45–46, **48**, 54, 62, 63, **85**
competition, 63, **69**, 80–81, 91
  See also stealing
conservation, 86, 89, 92–97, **94**, **96**, 100, **99**
courtship, 54, 63, 76, 95
crests, **43**, 44, 45, 60
crowned eagles, 66, 74

defenses, 54, 60, 78, 80–81, **82**
digestion, 57–58

diving, 8, **9**, 37, 67, **72**
double-clutching, 95, 97, 98

eating, 8, 30, 35, **35**, 38, 42, 45, 54, 57–58, 73, 80, 81
ecosystem, 100
eggs, 35, 78–79, 81, 90
endangerment, 46–49, 84–92, **87**, 97–100
evolution, 20–29, **21**, **22**, **23**, **24**, **25**, **28**
  bird ancestor, **23**, 26–27, **27**
  early eagles, 29
extinction, 27, 28, **28**, 29, 49, 91, **99**
eyelids, 56
eyesight, 10, 30, 55–56, 79

falconry, 18, **92**
feathers, 23, 26, **27**, 55, **59**, 59–63
  caring for, 60, **61**
  in fledging period, 63, 79, 81
  molting, 62, **62**, 63 See also
    color; crests; Native
    Americans; tails
feet. See legs and feet; talons
fish eagles, 20, 38–42, **39**, 55, **65**, 70, 98, 105 See also bald
  eagles
fledging period, 8–10, 38, 62, **62**, 63, 74, 79–83, **80**, **82**, **83**, **94**, 95
  post-fledging, 81–83
flight, 8, 10, 26, 37, 44–45, 57, 60, 66, 67, 70, 85
  first, 81, 83, **83**
  types of, 46, 66–67 See also
    anatomy; courtship
food, 8, 14, 20, **28**, 33–46, **35**, 68, 70–71, **71**
  poisoned, 86, 89–91

fossils, 20, **23**, 26

gender differences, 38–39, 44, 61, 63, 78–79
golden eagles, 10, 16, 18, 20, 33, 35–36, **36**, 66, 67, **69**, 69–70, 73, 76, 77, **77**, 97, 104
groups, **31**, 38, 42, 46, 49
  pairs, 46, 70, 76

Haast's eagle, 28
habitats, 33, 35, 37, 38, 41–42, 44, 45, 69–70, **71**–72, 79
  destruction of, 91–92, 93
hacking, 95, 98, 100
harpy eagles, 10, 33, 42–45, 42–45, **43**, 74, 91, **96**, 105
hawk-eagles, 37–38, **99**, 105
human beings
  beliefs, 10–19, **11**, **12**, **13**, **17**, 98
  as dangerous, 14, 16–17, 49, 84–92, **87**, **92** See also
    captivity; conservation
hunting, 32
  by eagles, 8, **9**, 37, 38, 41, 44, 46, **65**, 67, 69–70, 86
  of eagles, 14, 17–18, 46, 86, 89, 92–93

imperial eagles, **51**, 98, 104
Indian black eagle, 70, 104

legs and feet, **27**, 44, 45, 46, **52**, 54, **54**, 55, **55**, 79–80 See also talons
life span, 83, 86, **87**

metabolism, 57–58

migration, 10, 33, 36, 71–73, 86, 91, 92
molting, 62, **62**, 63
myths, 11–14, **12**, **13**, 17–18

Native Americans, 16–19, **19**, 86, **88**, 89
nests, 8, 35, 42, 44, 46, 49, 76–78, **77**
  artificial, 97
North America, 33, **34**, 37, 38, 73, 91–92

parenting, 8–10, 46, 49, 61, 63, 74, **75**, 78–81, **80**, 95, 97, 98

perches, 8, 67, 69
Philippine eagles, 44–45, 91, 97–98, **99**, 105, 106
poisoning, 86, 89–91, **90**
preening, 60, **61**
prey. *See* food

ranges, 33–49
  breeding, **34**, 71–72
reproduction, **34**, 58, 74, 76, 78–79, 95, 97

size, 10, 33, 36–49, 60–61, 63
snake eagles, 45–49, **47**, **48**, 55, 67, 69, 70, 106

species, 32, 33, 38, 42
  checklist, 104–106
  endangered, 49, 97–100, **99**
stealing, 38, 46, 70
Steller's sea-eagle, **41**, 41–42, 70, 105
symbolism, 10–11, **11**, **13**, 14–16, **15**, **17**, **19**

tails, 10, 57, 63, 64–66, **85**
talons, 8, 10, 30, 38, 44, 45, 54, **54**, **55**, 70

water, 58
Web sites, 107

About the Authors

TOM WARHOL has worked in the Science and Stewardship department of The Nature Conservancy, managing nature preserves in New Jersey and Massachusetts. He also volunteers at the Vermont Raptor Center, helping to care for injured eagles and other raptors. This is Tom's first book for this AnimalWays series; he is currently at work on AnimalWays: *Hawks*.

CHRIS REITER, who lives in rural West Virginia in a cottage much visited by wild creatures—bears, woodchucks, hummingbirds, bats, and flying squirrels among them—watches eagles and other raptors on the Potomac River. He has written several books on animals and the outdoors. His articles on preserving the natural world have appeared in *Natural History*, *Wild Earth*, and *Backpacker* magazines.